**Interior: Room**
**Exterior: City**

'Anthony Minghella . . . constantly tri
work to the Big Picture. Economics, sexuality, religion, ethnic
culture and family history all mesh together in dauntingly
complex ways . . . to determine, or at least deeply influence, the
fate of individuals in his plays. One of the joys of his intensely
lyrical writing is its close observation of the idiosyncracies of his
characters, and a deeply felt sense of their struggle, however
frustrated it may be, to move beyond the limitations imposed on
them by their history.' Paddy Woodworth, *Irish Times*

**Cigarettes and Chocolate** was first broadcast by BBC Radio 4 in
November 1988. It won the Best Drama Sony Award and Giles
Cooper Award for that year. 'One of the best radio plays I have
ever heard. Both in conception and execution it was profoundly
original.' B.A. Young, *Financial Times*

**Hang Up** was commissioned by the choreographer, Jonathan
Lunn, to accompany a dance duet first performed at the Sadler's
Wells Theatre in November 1987. The play was first broadcast on
BBC Radio 3 in November 1987 and won the Prix Italia for Radio
Fiction 1988 . 'An intense and brilliantly realized study of a love
affair.' Gillian Reynolds, *Daily Telegraph*

**What If It's Raining?** 'wonderfully depicts the difficulties of
grown-ups learning to be adults.' Mark Lawson, *Sunday Times*
'Has the attention-fixing properties of a razor blade in the sorbet.'
Geoffrey Phillips, *The Standard* 'This is television for grown-ups.'
John J. O'Connor, *New York Times*

**Anthony Minghella** was born in 1954 on the Isle of Wight of Italian
parents. He taught at the University of Hull until 1981. Since then
he has written for the stage, television, radio and film. His plays
include **Whale Music, A Little Like Drowning, Two Planks and a
Passion** and **Made in Bangkok**. His work has been highly
acclaimed in Europe and America. He was voted Most Promising
Playwright by the London Theatre Critics in 1984 who then
judged **Made in Bangkok** the Best Play of 1986. His series of nine
short films, **The Storyteller**, for Jim Henson and NBC won several
awards including an Emmy and a BAFTA Award.

**Methuen New Theatrescripts** series offers frontline intelligence of the most original and exciting work from the fringe.

*by the same author*

**Made in Bangkok**
**Whale Music & Other Plays**
(*Whale Music, A Little Like Drowning, Two Planks and a Passion*)

*Methuen/BBC Publication*

**Best Radio Plays of 1988**

# Interior: Room
# Exterior: City

## Cigarettes and Chocolate

## Hang Up

## What If It's Raining?

*Three Plays by*

*Anthony Minghella*

methuen

**A Methuen New Theatrescript**

*First published in Great Britain as a paperback original in the
Methuen New Theatrescript series in 1989 by Methuen Drama,
Michelin House, 81 Fulham Road, London SW3 6RB.
Distributed in the United States of America by HEB Inc,
70 Court Street, Portsmouth, New Hampshire 03801.*

**British Library Cataloguing in Publication Data**

Minghella, Anthony, *1954-*
      Interior:room exterior: city
      I. Title
      822'.914

      ISBN 0-413-61790-4

*Printed in Great Britain by Cox & Wyman Ltd, Reading*

*The front cover photograph shows Jonathan Lunn and Lauren Potter as*
He *and* She *in* **Hang Up.** *First performed by London Contemporary
Dance on 24 November 1987 at the Sadler's Wells Theatre.
(Photograph © Steve McMillan.)*

•

## Acknowledgements

My thanks to the rosary of names listed by each play who helped fashion the productions as they came to be broadcast. Appropriately, double thanks to the repeated names: Robert Cooper, whose guidance and friendship have been invaluable; and Juliet Stevenson, brilliant actress, brilliant accomplice, who would dignify my slightest line and has frequently done so.

I suppose it is fitting that **What if it's Raining?**, something of a painful chronicle, should have had such a difficult birth. It was commissioned by Granada Television, and despite the efforts and enthusiasm of June Howson and Howard Baker, seemed in danger of becoming marooned. I am much indebted to Louise Cooper for her perseverance in placing the trilogy long after my own energies had dimmed; to David Benedictus, then Commissioning Editor at Channel 4, for his role in fostering the project; and to the Producer, Mark Shivas, for his wit and wisdom, as well as his shrewdness in choosing Stephen Whittaker to direct the plays.

**Hang Up** was commissioned by the choreographer, Jonathan Lunn, to accompany a duet for himself and Lauren Potter for London Contemporary Dance Theatre. The play was subsequently broadcast on Radio 3 through the enterprise of Robert Cooper.

**Cigarettes and Chocolate** was commissioned by John Tydeman and Gordon House as part of BBC Radio's 1988 Globe Theatre Season.

Finally, thanks to Dominic Minghella for generously and rather foolishly shouldering the mammoth task of retyping and clarifying the text of **What If It's Raining?**; to Pamela Edwardes for suggesting and then navigating this volume; and to my wife, Carolyn Choa, who bunks and debunks with equal grace.

vi

## Introduction

Over the past four or five years I have found myself working on –
variously – a ballet, a short opera about kisses and science, a
fifteen minute television play about an expanding table, a
medieval comedy, a play set in Thailand, a clutch of detective
films, a series of short films dramatising European folk tales and a
radio play about a woman who stops talking.

The playwright working in the late eighties is besieged by
possibilities. I am always caught between admiration for those
writers who steadfastly operate in one medium, and what is, for
me, an irresistible temptation to explore all the available arenas
for my work. But then I suspect most playwrights are mavericks.
There is no austerity or privacy in our profession; that's for
novelists and poets. We must operate in the overcrowded room.
At the same time, the intensity which proceeds from the humanity
of drama, from the simple fact that its observations and analyses
are presented by actors, that there is the human voice, the human
action – whether it arrive across a stage, through a speaker, from a
flickering screen, down a square tube – grants the playwright
special powers. The current wisdom whereby theatre is deemed
the highest expression of this impure art is, I think, largely
historical phenomenon. The plays in this collection were written
either for radio or television. I regarded the making of them as no
less challenging or important than my work for the theatre.

I'm neither interested nor concerned with adjudicating the
behaviour of individuals; it has always seemed clear to me that
behaviour is primarily a reflection, albeit distorted, of society's
messages to its people. I don't sense this in any dark
conspiratorial sense; simply if we collectively opt for the
misanthropic, that's what we must surely get back.

The people in these plays can't communicate with each other, are
unfaithful and unhappy, and united in their search to give
meaning to their lives through careers, through acquisitions,
through art, through philanthropy, through therapy, through
affairs, through silence. They are increasingly cluttered. And
spiritually bankrupt. The writing is not so much satirical as
disappointed and impatient, both with its material and itself. For
the plays are as much a mirror held up to my own choices as they

are a reflection of the society in which I find myself. To borrow from Wilde, we live in a time which knows the price of everything and the value of nothing. And yet, amidst these accounts of failure of one kind or another, there is a yearning for something better, more decent, but not, perhaps, more civilised. The recurring weaknesses of human beings seem to me to be leavened by the potential for good, for laughter, for boundless generosity. And for love. And nothing which happens in the rooms of these plays makes sense without the activity outside of their windows.

**Anthony Minghella**
**London 1989**

There is a list
and it says
this person for doing this
and that person for doing nothing
and this person for not howling in rage
and that for desperately hanging on to the reasons the reasons
and
there is an avenger
who would be left?

from *In the Heart of the Beast* C. K. Williams

# Cigarettes and Chocolate

*for Kenny McBain 1946-89*

'I want it to go silent, it wants to go silent, it can't, it does for a second, then it starts again, that's not the real silence, it says that's not the real silence, what can be said of the real silence, I don't know . . .'

*The Unnameable,* Samuel Beckett

**Cigarettes and Chocolate** was first broadcast by BBC Radio 4 in November 1988, with the following cast:

| | |
|---|---|
| **Gemma** | Jenny Howe |
| **Rob** | Bill Nighy |
| **Lorna** | Juliet Stevenson |
| **Alistair** | Alex Norton |
| **Mother** | Joan Campion |
| **Gail** | Jane Gurnett |
| **Sample** | Christopher Ravenscroft |
| **Concepcion** | Sally Eldridge |

*Directed by* Robert Cooper and Anthony Minghella

## 1 Cigarettes and Chocolate

*Telephone ringing.*

**Gemma** (*a taped answerphone message*) Hello, you've rung 341 6293. If you'd like to leave a message for Gemma, please do so after you hear the tone.

*Tone. Then* **Gemma**'s *messages are heard.*

**Rob** It's me. Listen, did I leave my new toothbrush with you? The one with the, it's got a, you know, the big head . . . I think it was in your bag for some reason. Don't brush your hair with it. And don't open the olive oil, I need something to give my sister. Can I come round later for sex?

*Tone.*

**Lorna** Hi, it's me, are we on for tonight? Will you ring me before we meet and remind me to bring my glasses, because I can't read the subtitles without them. Two reviews are in favour, one against. Ring at seven, six forty-five, and say glasses. Ta ra.

*Tone.*

**Rob** It's Rob. I'm leaving home for the office, and I don't know what time I'll be home, late possibly, probably, probably ridiculously late. Best thing would be to stay with you otherwise I'll have to drive the extra seven hundred yards to my flat. Take pity on me.

*Tone.*

**Alistair** Gemma, look it's Alistair, you know, if you had anything from me this morning, you know, like a letter, don't read it, you know, if you haven't already opened, and if you have, if you have, if you have, don't think of it as a problem, you know, think of it as a not very good poem . . .

*Tone.*

**Mother** (*sceptical*) Gemma? It's your mother. Are you there? If you're there and not answering can you pick up the telephone? Gemma? I suppose you're out. Could you please telephone when you get in.

*Tone.*

**Rob** Rob. Two-thirty. I'm at work. Call me.

*Tone.*

**Gail** (*torrential*) Gemma, it's Gail. I hoped you'd be in because I wanted you to come and look at a flat with me. I'll read you the details, I can never remember whether your machine cuts you off after thirty seconds, I hope not because that drives me crazy, anyway, listen it's in, well the postcode is N19 but it's really Highgate Borders, I mean the Agents say Highgate which it isn't, but it's not inconvenient and anyway Highgate's ridiculous, as bad as you, it's impossible and this place has got a garden, it says pretty west-facing garden, although it doesn't say a length which is a bad sign, yesterday I saw a place in Camden with a Nice Town Garden, this is true, the details said Nice Town Garden and there was nothing, there wasn't one. There was a back yard where this guy had his bicycle and even that wouldn't stand straight, it was sort of bent up to squeeze it in.

*Cut off tone.*

Me again. I hate it when that happens. It makes you feel terrible, terribly rejecting, where was I? It's in Hornsey, did I say that, but I measured in the *A-Z* and it's really no further than, it's not as far north as Muswell Hill, say . . . it's about two inches above the Post Office Tower. I can't stand Muswell Hill. I hate the architecture as much as anything else: all those porches and it's smug, it's got smug porches. Will you come and look at this place with me? Two bedrooms, plus a bedroom/study so there's room for the baby, there'll be room for the baby, plus the garden as I said . . . reception: fireplace, cornices, 16′ x 11′ which is okay, and dado rails, dado rails, (*Pronounces the 'A' differently, first as in baby then as in far, then sing-song to the tune of 'Let's Call the Whole Thing Off '.*) You say Dado and I say Dado, whichever it is, who cares, so, I must hurry before I get cut off . . . I've got a scan at three tomorrow and I could go straight from that, so will you phone and let me know yes or no so I can make the appointment? It's much easier when you've got someone with, and Sample has a horror . . . actually if I could choose you'd come with me for the scan as well, would you hate

*Cut off tone.*

**Lorna**  It's Lorna, Gem, where are you? I'm in a callbox opposite the cinema. Are you on your way? Well, I'm assuming you're on your way. If for any reason you haven't left, I'll leave your ticket at the Box Office, or should I wait? There's a queue, Gem, and it's starting, what do I do?. Just hurry up, will you!

*Tone.*

**Rob**  It's Rob.

*Tone.*

# 3 Cigarettes and Chocolate

**Rob** *sighs, puts the phone down.*

*Tone.*

**Gemma**'s *flat. Morning.*

*We hear the sounds of a spring morning in England. Larks, grasshoppers. Music begins, opening bars from Bach's 'Matthew Passion'. But we might feel we're hearing it through open french windows, because* **Gemma** *is speaking from her small, walled garden in North London.*

**Gemma** The day I stopped talking was one of those perfect days we have in England. They come in the spring and in the autumn, differently, the one full of entrance the other full of exit, but the same in the way the air thins and you can see the edge of everything. And somehow green is more green, blue more blue. I wish I'd had another week, but there it was, a big red cross on my calendar, and everything was ready . . . I'd had my holiday, in Italy, wonderful, wonderful, as if I'd put my tongue on a small pile of salt . . . or a glass of wine. Italy was a glass of dark wine swilled in the mouth. And I'd spoken to them all, in turn, carefully, loving them all, like suicide in a way: to stop talking. Like killing oneself.

*Music and garden out.*

*Interior cafe, day time.*

*Cafe with sophisticated background music, jazz or similar.*

**Rob** Hi, have you been waiting?

**Lorna** No.

**Rob** Am I always late?

**Lorna** I think so, yes.

**Rob** Yes, I think I am. Not very good is it?

**Lorna** I adjust. Your coffee's cold. Actually, I don't think you were late in the beginning.

**Rob** You look nice. I'm supposed to be at a meeting.

**Lorna** Really, and what? What? Do you mean –?

**Rob** I'm not going. I made some excuse. Sod it.

**Lorna** What? You were meeting your lover?

**Rob** Exactly. That's exactly what I said.

**Lorna** I can believe that.

**Rob** Lorna, she's stopped talking.

**Lorna** What? Who?

**Rob** Gemma! She's not talking. I went there this morning and she had just ceased to talk, she won't answer the telephone, she won't return calls, she won't say a single word to me.

**Lorna** Why?

**Rob** Well, obviously, because of this . . .

**Lorna** Why? Did you tell her?

**Rob** No.

**Lorna** Well I certainly haven't told her.

**Rob** She's very intuitive, she's very acute about these things.

**Lorna** Really? I wouldn't have said so.

**Rob** I'm telling you.

**Lorna** I've just been on holiday with you both and we managed to –

**Rob** There's no need to –

**Lorna** I'm not being anything, I'm just pointing out –

**Rob** I didn't say you were being anything – anyway, let's –

**Lorna** Would you rather we stopped seeing each other?

**Rob** No.

**Lorna** What then?

**Gail** Rob!

**Rob** Gail! Hi! Hi! Lorna and I are having an assignation! Ignore us!

**Gail** Oh hi, Lorna, I didn't realise it was you, wonderful coat, is that new? Where's Tom?

**Lorna** It's ancient, it is nice though, isn't it? Sit down. Tom's with Gerti. (*The Nanny.*) Have you met Gerti?

**Gail** I thought it was Anna?

**Lorna** No, Anna's gone. Gerti's wonderful.

**Gail** Can she speak English?

**Lorna** She's Danish. She speaks better English than me.

**Rob** Have some coffee.

**Gail** I thought you were off coffee for Lent?

**Rob** This is mostly froth.

**Lorna** Have some froth. You look wonderful.

**Gail** Thanks. I've put on fourteen-and-a-half pounds.

**Rob** (*to the* **Waitress**) Excuse me, could we have another coffee? Actually, I'll have another, make it three could you? Cappucino. Thanks a lot.

**Gail** Any more I'm going to have to make bras out of duffle bags.

**Lorna** Is it going well?

**Gail** Apparently. The amniocentesis was, you know, clear.

**Lorna** Terrific. So do you know what sex it is?

**Gail** I do, Lorna, but I've got to keep it a secret. Sample doesn't want to know.

**Lorna** Right.

**Gail** How's Stephen? What are you two doing here?
Is this really an assignation?

**Rob** Seriously.

**Gail** How exciting. Is a threesome out of the question?

**Rob** Jump in.

**Gail** How's Gemma?

**Rob** She's great.

**Gail** She doesn't ring back when you leave a message on that bloody machine. What's the matter with her, the old bag? I wanted her to come and look at some places with me. I've only discovered this cafe since I've been flat-hunting. It's really nice, isn't it?

**Rob** Yeah.

**Gail** I know what I wanted to ask you, Lorna . . . (*Deflected.*) Look at you both, I forgot you were all in Italy together, look at you, it's not the coat, well it is the coat, but it's the colour . . . it's February and you've both caught the sun! Was it wonderful?

**Rob** It was. Tom was wonderful. The grown-ups were okay. Stephen cheated at Scrabble.

**Lorna** So did you.

**Rob** I cheated openly. Stephen pretended he wasn't. I always cheat. If you always cheat, it's hardly cheating at all, is the way I look at it.

**Gail** Did Gemma have a good time? Oh God, you pigs, I love Italy.

**Lorna** Gemma was fine. Political.

**Rob** She wasn't political.

**Lorna** She wanted to adopt a Vietnamese baby we saw outside the Uffizi.

**Gail** Why?

**Lorna** Why, Rob?

**Rob** That's not fair. The context was . . . that's not fair, Lorna. It was because we were having such a good time.

**Gail** I'm having a nice time I think I'll adopt that Vietnamese boy? Was he up for sale?

**Rob** No. No, of course not. No, he had Dutch parents. At least we assumed they were Dutch. They wore those funny shoes that you can get in Covent Garden: so ugly you can convince yourself they're good for you. Only Dutch people wear them.

**Gail** You mean clogs?

**Rob** Not clogs. Those shoes which look like somebody ran over a pair of Nature Treks. And they had this Vietnamese boy, extraordinarily beautiful. (*Consulting* **Lorna**.) Wasn't he? (*To the* **Waitress** *who's arrived with the coffees.*) Thanks. Do you want anything else, Gail? We could get you up to fifteen pounds if you're interested.

**Lorna**  I'm going to have to get my skates on shortly.

**Rob**  Really? Should I cancel the hotel room?

**Lorna**  (*saying 'Yes'*)  Sorry.

**Gail**  I'm completely confused about this Dutch Vietnamese boy.

**Rob**  Ask Gemma. It was her idea. She just said, actually she didn't just say – she went on about it all night. Did I tell you this, Lorna? You know we carried on the conversation the entire night? She kept saying 'How much do we give back? Expressed as a percentage of what we have: how much do we give back?'

**Gemma**'s *flat. Evening. Bach's 'Matthew Passion'.*

**Alistair**  Oh God, Gemma, I feel terrible now, I'm going to have to tell the others, I'm going to have to tell Rob, I'm going to get my wee nose bloodied, this love I have for you, this love I mentioned in my letter, it's not a big obstacle type of love, it's not a trip over me on your front doorstep type of love, it's not a, it's small, it's a kind of very irrelevant passion, it was hardly worth writing down, it started off as a p.s. and got bigger in the letter, I'm speaking of proportion, I love you in brackets is what I was saying, oh-by-the-way type of thing; on a scale of one to ten, you know: one-and-a-half when I'm feeling really badly about it, it's a hot water bottle, 'I'm feeling terrible but at least Alistair loves me', when the fellow walks out on you, 'You're by yourself Gemma but at least that little chappie nurses a crushette I can cry on his shoulder while I wait for Mr Right to come along' it was not, repeat not, block capitals IT WAS NOT INTENDED TO MAKE YOU STOP TALKING TO EVERYONE! Oh God, Gemma.

*A Restaurant. Day.*

**Rob**  Italy. Italy was the trouble, was where it started, I realise that now, this wonderful restaurant we kept going to, we went with Stephen and Lorna and Tom who's their, who's two or something, well you know Tom anyway . . . Sample, have I told you this?

**Sample**  I don't think so, was this when –?

**Rob**  (*ploughing on*)  The food was, God, the first time we went they brought, there was no menu, they just brought food to the table . . . – *do you want these mushrooms? Fantastic wild mushrooms,* –

and there was fish, really fresh, these people were terrific, we kept
going back, you could see the river from the table, oh God, it was
a great holiday. Gemma was, she had the best time, we were
talking about kids, she kept holding Tom and, who's really nice,
in as much as a two year old, although they, Stephen's always
making him wear these ridiculous, but he's remarkable, in the
restaurant, perfect, of course that's the Italians they make you feel
as if anything is perfectly, so no, and then she (*Distracted suddenly.*)
Do you notice the central heating?

**Sample**  I don't know. I'm not cold. Are you cold?

**Rob**  No. No. I'm hot. I'm too hot. Is it on?

**Sample**  I expect so. It's February. I expect it's on. Feel the
radiator. It's just behind you.

**Rob**  Well it isn't on. As it happens. I don't know, but there's
vestigial central heating, do you know what I mean? The plants.
The plants here are dying of it, and they're just plants, imagine
what it's doing to us, I really noticed that when we came back
here, of course the first thing you notice is the traffic which is now
ridiculous, it is ridiculous, imagine a Martian . . . the traffic, the
streets, I think that must be a strike, I'm sure it's not absence
which had made them so dirty, not my absence, our absence, but
the absence of street cleaners. My flat when I got back, outside, –
you know the place outside where we leave the rubbish – so you
arrive and wade through the armadas of black bags, well there's
somebody who lives in the flats who clearly has psychopathic
tendencies, really, during the election somebody delivered a
Labour Party car sticker and it was in my letter box, you know
where the letter rack is, with the dominoes, you know where the
dominoes are . . .

**Sample**  (*he does*)  I love that, was that your idea?

**Rob**  It might have been the psychopath who used the dominoes,
must have been when I came to think of it, you have to have a
psychopathic turn of mind to use dominoes to number the letter
boxes, so anyway I get home in the evening and the sticker is still
there in my letter box, except now it's in a thousand little pieces,
literally, thousands of little pieces, which is psychopathic.

**Sample**  (*agreeing*)  God. (*Pause.*) Gemma hates your flat, doesn't
she, because of that, because she said the people who live there,
the other people, she's always saying that, the Porsches . . .

**Rob**  (*irritated*)  There's only one Porsche, the secretary of the

Labour Party lives there as well as it happens, she's always doing that . . . there's only one Porsche in the entire building. It's a left-hand drive, it's an old left-hand drive Porsche, it's actually rather beautiful. Of course it's revolting. It's full of revolting people. You know, but it's very beautiful, and it's got the park. When you've been somewhere healthy you really appreciate that, somewhere sane, even fresh air, even that is no longer freely available. Even that's political. My point is, about the flat, my flat, is that with this strike, I'm assuming it is a strike, instead of being careful, the psychopath has lost all self-control and has abandoned the black bag regime . . . you know they won't take the rubbish unless it's in black bags? Well that's all out of the window and there's this kind of deluge of little shopping bags, plastic carrier bags with stuff spilling out, bits of pizza and God knows what, the guy clearly is the Take Away king of North London, when they catch him there will be serious economic problems in the Indian Restaurant trade, and it's all there, the evidence, and each time I get home I want to kill him, I want to wade in to his little plastic bags and discover his name, I know somewhere between the polystyrene and foil containers, between the Chicken Tikka Masala and the, I'm sure there's abandoned pornography as well, stuff which is delivered in plain brown envelopes, there are a lot of bits of plain brown envelopes and stuff from American Express, there will be his name, he will have left his name somewhere on an envelope, and once I've found it I intend to scoop up an armful of this crap which is now blocking the entrance to the flats, you have to climb over it, you have to queue up with the vermin, the cockroaches, the queues of parasites who are racing up the hill to the feast, I am going to scoop up the worst of this crap and ring his bell and dump it over his mentally deranged psychopathic little head.

**Sample**  That's awful. Because it's a beautiful flat.

**Rob**  I know, I'm really lucky, I'm really blessed to have it. I feel terrible. All my friends come round, this is my paranoia, my friends come round and they think sod him.

**Sample**  I always think that. I think sod him for having such a terrific flat.

**Rob**  Except Gemma. Who hates it.

**Sample**  Well, I expect she means the windows. Because there aren't really any windows.

**Rob** (*raging*)  Of course there are windows! There are loads of windows!

**Sample** (*conciliatory*) I suppose she – I love it, I keep telling you, I love it, I'll swap – but you know she loves light.

**Rob** I love light! This makes me really angry. She doesn't have copyright on liking light. Light is very important to me, and my flat is often very light, but she does this, she makes a decision about something and that's it, finished, my flat has no light and is full of Porsches. If she'd agree to live with me, which after all this time is one of the more tired jokes among our friends, right? If she'd move in with me we could buy somewhere really special which was all windows if that is what she wants, we could buy a huge greenhouse and make babies, Vietnamese babies if that's what she wants, that's another thing I have to tell you about, the Vietnamese baby . . . Christ . . . her place is not that light as it happens and it's damp and then she has the central heating, this is my point, this is what I was saying just now . . . she has the central heating up full blast and then everyone feels ill all the time. Since we got back from Italy I have felt ill, physically ill, all the time, which is what's wrong with her, probably, something as simple as the central heating and instead of turning it down, turning it off, or agreeing to buy a flat with me, she has this whatever it is, this . . . what do you think it is? I don't know. She won't speak to me. Has she spoken to you? She hasn't spoken to anyone. Has she said anything to you? Has she said anything to Gail?

**Sample** Nothing. No. I don't think so.

**Rob** Well, if she does: tell her to turn the central heating off. Sample, honestly, she has not said a word to anyone for a week. I mean, it's ridiculous. Now she's turned her machine off. The phone just rings and rings.

*Phone ringing and ringing.*


**Gemma**'s *flat. Evening.*

**Gail** *with* **Gemma**, *music. Bach's 'Matthew Passion'.*

**Gail** Sample says I'm to mention the central heating to you although I can't think why, it's not on is it? Is it because there's something wrong with your central heating and because you're not speaking you can't do anything about it? Why don't you write down something on a piece of paper? That wouldn't compromise you would it? Is it a love affair? Who is it? Or is Rob fooling around? I have to tell you Lorna and I and Sample spent an entire evening on Friday speculating, your ears must have been burning! It's a great way to become the centre of attention, that's my problem I talk too much and then nobody's interested, although I think you could say a few words and still be mysterious, if it's a bit of mystery you're after. Anyway, for the record: I thought you **were having an affair, Lorna thought it was Rob, I mean something to do with Rob, – I'm trying to read your face, Gem,** you're so inscrutable! It's not the baby, is it? It's not my baby, is it? (*She thinks it might be.*) I don't think it is. I can't think it could be that. I know you – I know that's something you'd eventually, but, (*Doesn't pursue it.*) I can't remember what Sample thought, if indeed he did think, impending fatherhood is making him all sort of fey and gloomy and concerned, I can't get him to come anywhere near me, he's gone all reverent which is a bit ridiculous, I think he's given me up for Lent, I'm only eighteen weeks. Anyway I know you think I'm too smutty, to tell you the truth, Gem, it'll be quite nice not to feel obliged to every five minutes; I mean enough is enough, particularly if you're sort of saying we'll be doing this for donkey's years. It's like serving up spaghetti bolognese every night. Who needs it? I mean I like my spag. bol. as much as the next girl, that is not my point, this is what I was trying to say to Sample last night, I don't know how it started as he's even started coming to bed in track suit bottoms, but probably because I said something like 'this is nice holding hands', which'll teach me for not saying what I thought which was, you know, 'I won't break', but he said something like 'I hope you don't like it more than our wild nights of passion,' Well! apart from I imagine your finding it as tricky as I do to imagine Sample in a wild night of anything, he can be very sweet to me, I mean for God's sake I love the bloke, I'm having his baby, so the point is last night he starts sulking right after I've lied about liking holding hands with him in his track suit bottoms and me in my sleep bra and so he starts this huge sulk about us never doing it ever again because he's got the calendar out by this time and is sort of saying well it's at least five months after this and ten weeks after that and stitches, which of course puts the fear of God up me and before you know it we're both really miserable but to tell you the truth I'm quite relieved because it means, I mean do you know anybody, any woman, who deep down, I mean really deep down under the first deep down where you admit to being insatiably lustful about everybody, what I'm saying is under that layer have you met anybody who actually would rather, I mean I'm not saying to begin with then you're courting and sorting out whether or not he fancies you, he's got to not be able to keep his hands off you at that stage, then that's fine: up the stairs, in the back of the Renault, every five minutes, I mean great, that's sort of required, but once you've said to yourself 'okay you'll do' well it's what I said about the old spag. bol. isn't it? See! if you don't shut me up look what happens! Tell you the truth, Gem, I'm getting a bit worked up about this baby, it's the hormones, obviously, look, these are all new, I never had a mark on my face, that's one thing I've always had is my skin, Gem, you know I may nót be a beauty but I've always had fantastic skin, that's not vanity, and now suddenly look at all that and I just know I'm going to have stretch marks like a deflated balloon, which is fine, but that's always been my strong point, Gem, you know so it seems bloody unfair, but that's not it anyway, it's just I've been pregnant before, right, so now I've said, oh shit, not a big deal I have been pregnant before, I expect if the chips were down I'm not alone in this, which is neither here nor there, you know I'm not one of those women who, (*She's crying.*) you know I was speaking to this American woman the other day who has got everything, pool in the garden, holidays in Hawaii and she kept saying – you don't know her, it's got nothing to do with a swimming pool, she kept saying 'fill your house up with babies, Gail, fill your house with babies, like flowers . . .', great, I haven't even got a flat yet, and if I do I'll fill it with myself and – because Sample won't live there, will he? I mean he's never wanted to live with me before, so . . . I'm just saying the abortion thing which I'd do again if it were the same circumstances because I was like a kid at the time myself, I mean I wasn't a kid according to my passport, but in every other respect and the guy would have run a mile, of course, which all just goes to making this baby very important, because I can feel it and it feels like a big sob in my stomach, all day I keep thinking it's there like this great sobbing in my stomach . . . fill your house with babies, like flowers . . . I think you should say something, Gemma, because it's not fair is it, all these confessions, I bet you're getting all these wonderful confessions, is there a tape recorder? Have you seen the size of my tits? Pretty impressive, eh? Anyway, I've passed on the stuff about the central heating. Do you think anybody could survive in Holloway, I mean off the Holloway Road? I don't think so. (*Bleak.*) Actually, it's bloody awful.

*The music plays.*

*Soho Office. Day*

**Alistair**'s *office.* **Alistair** *and* **Rob**.

**Rob** How could anyone so beautiful do that to himself? I swear, Al. That is what she said. Those were her words. Such a beautiful face. How could he set fire to himself? I have to say it made me pretty angry.

**Alistair** What? That the monk was beautiful?

**Rob** No, come on: Gemma. Come on. I got angry with her, because there we were, the entire day poisoned, and I thought well okay, this monk has done this to himself and he felt that was important. Obviously, I mean, obviously he felt it was crucial or something, it was obviously not just a gesture, and so fine it screws up all our plans and we send everybody home, including my sister who already thinks Gem is, and okay it's important, but then she says such a beautiful face and I'm afraid that made me furious. And she's got him up on her noticeboard, the beautiful self-immolator, and frankly, Alistair, I almost burned his photograph with my lighter.

**Alistair** Why? I don't follow. Because she thought he was beautiful? Sorry Rob, I don't follow you.

**Rob** I'm just saying we're talking about a woman who went to Greenham Common, okay, which is fine by me, great, but she has to drive back here and find out where Greenham Common is on the map. That's all.

**Alistair** And?

**Rob** Well, you know, if you're going to have principles, Alistair, buy yourself a map and a noticeboard.

**Alistair** If I'm getting your gist you're complaining because Gemma didn't know where Greenham Common was before she went there, or that she was upset when a beautiful monk committed suicide because of what was happening in Tibet . . . am I right, pal? I mean she knew Greenham Common was in England. That would do for me. Or do you need a woman with Geography 'A' Level?

**Rob** And what's all this about? The silence? I mean what is all that about?

**Alistair** (*thrown*) I don't know, Rob. I mean if you don't know. (*Shrugs.*) I don't know.

**Rob** Italy. Italy must have something to do with it. And the Vietnamese baby. Who was probably Dutch. (*Despairing.*) You know. I can't go round there, Alistair. I can't bear all that music. The 'Matthew Passion'. I keep thinking it must be a clue. Have you been round? Does your ioniser have any effect do you think? I lie in my room with mine in my mouth. You can get tiny electric shocks on the tongue.

**Alistair** You should talk to Concepcion.

**Rob** Should I? Who's Concepcion? I thought your cleaner was called Concepcion?

**Alistair** That's right. She's my cleaner. She's terrific. She's a psychiatrist.

**Rob** Great. What? You mean she has insight and stuff? You talk to her? What are you talking about, Alistair?

**Alistair** I just said, she's a psychiatrist. She trained as a psychiatrist in Argentina. She's only a cleaner in London. In Argentina she's a psychiatrist.

**Rob** Your cleaner is a psychiatrist.

**Alistair** That's right. I've told you before, actually. She's amazing. I get my shirts ironed by an amazingly beautiful Argentinian psychiatrist.

**Rob** Listen, would you mind if I opened the window, I find it difficult to breathe in here, do you notice that? I think it's just very stuffy at the moment. How can you work in here with all these dead plants? (*Opens window to a deluge of traffic.*) I got clamped this morning. You can't drive off. Nothing happens. I thought I'd just drive off with that notice in front of my face, on the three wheels. But you can't. It is pointless driving in London. There is absolutely no point. There is man directly below your office in a very big car and because the traffic has clearly unhinged him, he is stuck sideways across the road. His nose is touching a parked BMW and his tail is touching another parked BMW. In about two sec – the blue BMW has a dent . . . and now so does the black one . . . (*We hear the appropriate clunks and thuds and engine chorus.*)
blue 2 black 1
blue 3 black 1
blue 3 black 2
(*Car squeals off.*) and off to the gym, to the T'ai Chi, to the aromatherapy, to the . . .

**Alistair**  No, I've got this great deal going with Concepcion because I'm paying her three fifty an hour right? Which is not cheap but is the going rate for domestic help, so fine, but thrown in I get a little therapy, it's limited vocabulary therapy, but I get to talk over the vaccuum cleaner or the washing machine, I feel everything's being tidied up at once. It's a wonderful deal. I've made all sorts of discoveries.

**Rob**  Such as?

**Alistair**  Such as the vaccuum cleaner whistles when the bag is full, such as you put a tennis ball in the washing machine for some obscure but deeply helpful reason, such as I harbour this desire to murder my cousin. Which was not a discovery but I've owned up to it. No, Concepcion is perfect, or would be if she would sleep with me.

**Rob**  Sounds great. Which cousin?

**Alistair**  Such as I am in love with Gemma.

**Rob**  She told you this, or you told her?

**Alistair**  I'm serious, Rob. I wrote to Gemma and told her. I had to. I know it's not how you treat your mates but this was serious. I wrote her a letter, not a big deal or anything, you know, in the third paragraph of this wee note, and next thing she's not speaking to anyone.

**Rob**  Alistair, only you and your psychiatric cleaner didn't know you were in love with Gemma, it's got nothing to do with your letter. I don't mean to belittle the depth of feeling and, but it has nothing to do with this confession.

**Alistair**  Right.

**Rob**  Because Gemma knew, is what I am saying. She knew. You wear it on your sleeve, you come to dinner and it's 'Could you pass the wine, Gemma, and I'm in love with you'. 'Oh Gemma, do you really think so and I'm in love with you.' 'Gemma, fantastic kidney beans and I'm in love with you'. So listen: don't feel badly because it's fine, Alistair, really, and I'm delighted you're in love with her, it made her feel nice, I'm sure it still does, she's probably a little bit in love with you.

**Alistair**  Yeah, but you know Rob I really love her. Oh God. I cried when I told Concepcion. Oh God, it was just the relief of admitting it. I think I'm going to cry again now which would be embarrassing, I am not famous in this office for laughing on the

wrong side of my face as my dad would say. Don't laugh on the
wrong side of your face, son. Oh.

**Gemma**'s flat. Evening.

The 'Matthew Passion'.

**Rob** I am actually very aggravated, you know. I find it very
aggravating. I find it childish, I find it shocking and aggressive,
very aggressive, actually, because you know what it says to me
Gem
because by all means don't speak to the world,
go right ahead.
but with me, it says, I include you with the
others, I exclude you from anything private,
or intimate or
plus, I'm pretty certain I know what, why,
what's behind all of this, and I feel like
I'm being put in the stocks for it
so, if there is a problem, instead of talking about it
you

The music plays.

I don't know if you're eating, or sleeping,
I don't know what you're thinking.

The music plays.

**Rob** is suddenly agitated.

what?
and please don't stare at that bloody
photograph!
because you know I have a particular
antipathy towards that picture, we've been
through this.
I don't think it's very clever, or brave, or
effective, or real, or real! to set fire to
yourself,
in fact, it's very similar,
what you're doing, what he's doing.
it's very similar,
it's like a kind of major sulk, isn't it?
in fact, I am going to burn that picture,
I should have done this the last time,

*He rips the photograph off the notice board*
*holds it up threateningly –*

well talk to me then, talk to me, talk to me

*Pause.*

okay.
okay.

*He sets fire to the photograph with his lighter.*

this is just so . . .

*It burns.*

sod it
look, I'll get you another picture, I shouldn't have
done that.
I shouldn't have done that
you know, but I'm frustrated. I'll find the photograph and get you
another one.
I'm sorry, I shouldn't have done that.
Look, I'll go.

*Pause.*
*The music plays,* **Rob** *sighs.*

Gemma

*The music plays.*

Gemma?

*The music plays.*


**Gemma**'s *flat. Morning. The 'Matthew Passion'.*

**Alistair** *and* **Gemma** *are listening. The work finishes. We hear applause.*

**Alistair**  No, I like it. I'm really getting to like it.

*The recording starts again. Side one of a piece which is very, very long..*

**Alistair**  (*taking a deep breath. The price of love*)  Again? Great. Great.

*He hums and half sings.*

**Alistair**  Terrific.

**Alistair**'s flat. Day.

**Rob** to **Concepcion. Concepcion** is ironing.

**Rob** Is it . . . do you mind if . . . I . . . I should have brought my shirts round . . . I'll give you an example. This is one, there are loads of others. We had a visitor from the States, and we'd taken him out, we'd taken him to the South Bank, no what it was, sorry, we had collected this guy from Heathrow, and it was this time last year, actually, it was Good Friday, and this guy had arrived from San Francisco and was completely jet-lagged, but what had happened was that Gemma had gotten us tickets for the 'Matthew Passion' at the Festival Hall and didn't want to miss it, if you knew her you'd understand because it's like a very important thing, annual event to go there and she sits with the score and is completely . . . music gives her something which I certainly could never, I look at her sometimes when she's listening to music and I'm frightened, I feel lonely, I'm frightened because it's a lover's face, and I never really see it . . . would you mind if I just opened the window a little? I think it's the iron, the steam, am I speaking too fast for you? sorry, I'm sure I'm completely incoherent . . .

**Concepcion** (*heavy accent*) No, no . . . you were at a concert with an American friend . . . it's okay, I'll do the window.

**Rob** Well, of course, you'll know about jet lag and this guy he was very game and sort of sat there propped up, but I don't know if you know the 'Matthew Passion', it's not short, it is in fact the opposite of short, it is fantastically long. I mean it goes on and on you get an interval of about two hours, it's a marathon, okay? but of course wonderful, even I see that. Gem's always saying it has more good tunes in that one piece than in the rest of, it's great, and she's there following every bar in her book while this poor American guy is sitting bolt upright and then every now and then swaying and then catching himself and going back to upright, then lurching, then swaying, then bolt upright in this terrible torture of staying awake . . .

**Concepcion** Uhuh.

**Rob** . . . and then we get to the interval and go off to find some food, because I also realise this guy must be famished, Alistair won't mind if I take a cup of tea, will he?

**Concepcion** Sure.

**Rob** He's eaten me out of house and home many a time, so I'm sure he won't . . . I think I'll pinch a banana, it's ripe anyway, so, mmm, actually I'll just have juice, I'm not supposed to be drinking tea, is there any herb? No look: juice is fine, great, so anyway, where was I? This is really nice of you, you know.

**Concepcion**  It's no problem.

**Rob**  (*flirting a little*)  I'd really like to, I really appreciate it, I do. (*Tails off.*) Where were we? Oh yes, so we toddle off to find something to eat, and it's now the middle of the afternoon and our American friend is sleep-walking and we get to some patio or other, with all kinds of things going on, do you know the South Bank? by the NFT and the National Theatre, well there's always stuff going on, clowns and those funny dancers and stalls and stuff and buskers and this is all great for Felix, the American, who, – 'cause there he is first time in London and he can see the Thames and all the monuments – and we queue up for ages and get sandwiches and sit out in the sunshine having, eating, and getting some fresh air before plunging back into the Passion, which of course is now getting very heavy and moving and stuff, so like it's a very welcome break and Felix is reviving a little with the food and there's buskers playing, a really nice flautist. I can see it so vividly, this guy comes round with a cap to collect for this flautist, who's really wonderful, beautiful sound and you know what it's like sometimes when you're in the fresh air and there's music playing it's really lovely and with a glass of wine and so of course I dug into my pocket and gave a pound or something, some money for this flautist who's probably a student at the Royal College, I think it's standard practice for them to go out and busk and stuff, so . . . I give him some money and then we carry on eating and I'm not alone in this there are loads of people there from the concert, too, all eating and being entertained and they all give generously and . . . anyway the point is about ten minutes later, maybe five minutes, or even sooner, I can't quite remember, anyway I don't know if you know that area but it's a real haven for dossers, you know: down and outs, there are lots of people down by Waterloo Station, homeless, who can't get accommodation, it's really awful of course, you drive by at night and there are these huge fires, particularly in the winter, there are a lot of people there, there are a lot of homeless people . . . I'm sure you know all about this, and what happens of course is that one of these people, a woman, who had a drink problem, I mean she was carrying a bottle of cider and she had on a duffle coat and she smelt and, of course – it wasn't her fault, but you can't help those people by giving them a pound coin, you know, because they go and buy a bottle of cider and get pissed and it's not helping, so I didn't respond to this woman, and obviously, it was awkward for Felix, because she kept kind of pestering him, he looked, you know how all Americans look wealthy, they sort of exude dollars, and I was quite firm, I suppose, and anyway, this woman went off, in fact I did give her 50p, as it happens, but it was just to get rid of her, I really feel strongly that it wasn't helping her in the slightest, it was just another dousing of the liver, I gave her 50p and in fact she looked disgusted, she looked so disgusted I wished I'd just ignored her . . . so . . . and Gem is watching all this and saying nothing and we finish our food and we go back to the concert, of course as I'm telling you this the symbolism is all absolutely transparent but at the time, as we wander back to the concert I'm thinking about Felix, who is going a kind of pale grey at the prospect of another two hours of Bach: you know I find it quite a strain to sit through however wonderful but we go back in and all the singers stand up and of course it's riveting in a way – no, it's wonderful, – and Felix does fall asleep and then it finishes and we're on our way back to the car, – great banana thanks, I was just a little peckish – and Gemma starts wandering around this area looking as if she's lost something, which would not be unusual, and so I stand there holding Felix up, Felix has by this time given up pretending to be with us, he is in rapid eye movement dreaming of futons and California and sanity and Gemma is hunting around the back of benches and – sort of urgent and anxious and uncommunicative – and then she walked down a side road by the Cut, near the station and sure enough, by one of these huge open fires, the clusters of tramps, getting near the violent hour, the windscreen smashing hour, the abuse hour, Gemma wanders amongst these people poking around in their sacks and their sleeping bags and their cardboard boxes and yes there is our lady from the interval, settling down with her cider in a black dustbin liner filled with newspaper, essentially we'd walked into somebody's bedroom, I tried to make this point later, unsuccessfully, and Gem bends down and starts talking to her, 'What's your name? Where do you live?' I'm not joking. 'Where do you live?' and she said, of course, 'I live here.' Her name was Muriel. 'I'm Gemma', says Gemma 'and this is Rob and this is our friend Felix. Are you hungry, Muriel?' Muriel was hungry. 'Let me give you some money. Muriel, I'm going to give you ten pounds, okay, and I want you to go and buy yourself a meal.' And out comes this ten pound note. Ten pounds to the Muriels of this world is not a note, it is a pale hot liquid in a big bottle. It is half an hour of a delicious burning sensation. It is not a meal. So I say this, I am, of course, embarrassed and uncomfortable and I am propping up Felix who would not turn a hair before slipping in beside Muriel in the black plastic bag. Actually what I am is furious, I am choking with anger. 'Okay', says Gemma, who has gone that kind of, you know what it feels like to write with a pencil just after you've sharpened it, like that, like that is how she went, she yanked Muriel out of the sack and then we were wandering along the South Bank, because Gemma was going to find Muriel a place where she could have a meal, which we would supervise. Felix hasn't spoken for about seven hours, he's disappeared into his jacket, he's asleep in his pocket, Gemma walks purposefully staring ahead dragging Muriel, who is leaning on me, stinking to high heaven, like a hung rabbit, like a jugged hare, I can still smell that . . . ach! anyway, and Muriel is saying 'I'm thirsty, I'm a bit thirsty, where are we?' and she pulls out her little bottle of liquor from one of her many carrier bags which have devolved into my safe keeping and is about to swig from it when down comes Gemma's avenging hand, yanks this full bottle from Muriel and sends it flying into the Thames. We listen in silence as it hit the water. Splash.

Restaurants won't serve the homeless, or drunks, it puts customers off, they see the bags, they smell the jugged hare and they're suddenly fully booked or closing or don't speak English. Eventually we are in the car, driving in to the West End. Gemma has begun speaking about taking Muriel home and giving her a bath, giving her some clothes, oh God, listen Concepcion: I admire her, I love her, she's extraordinary, she really does, she means what she's saying, and I admire her, you know but she's also a complete pain in the neck and the car is like a medieval kitchen and Felix is getting car sick and Gemma is getting into a rage, we stop at one restaurant which is empty and has WE ARE OPEN UNTIL TWO across its lights, the sign, the façade, and suddenly it's out of food, and Gemma starts yelling and kicks out at one of the tables and Muriel is crying and the manager of this place is ringing the police and it's all very ugly and Felix is sitting in the back seat of the car, perched with his head in his hands and his stomach emptying into the pavement and back go Muriel's bags and Muriel in beside him and I'm driving along with Gemma consoling Muriel who is crying and Felix groaning and I can feel this violence uncoiling inside me and then Muriel says 'I want to come and live with you.' and again we all listen in silence as this hits the water. Splash.

We drove to the nearest Macdonalds, bought her a Big Mac with everything on it and left her there eating it. She was about three miles from where she lived and it was after midnight. She had beautiful eyes. I suppose she was fifty, she could have been any age, I suppose she could have been forty or fifty or sixty, but she had these beautiful grey eyes and they rested on you as you spoke. And hoped. With such longing. Whenever I've witnessed atrocities on television, people starving, tortured, degraded, abandoned, they've always had Muriel's eyes, and the same look: Disappointed. I can't think of a better way of describing the look. Just disappointed. Disappointed.

**Gemma**'s *flat. Evening.*

*The 'Matthew Passion'.*

**Lorna** It's like uh . . . this is like therapy, isn't it? . . .
I hate analysis, I hate, I hate the idea of undressing myself, you know, like making love with a stranger, worse, worse than that, actually.

We went, Stephen and I, we both went, we went together, that was to a counsellor and then we went to see different people, separately, in fact.

I was very humiliated, I was, it was very humiliating for me, so I, well I've told you, Gemma, about the sunbed, going for my sunbed, in fact I've got my own sunbed, which I hide, I've got my own sunbed, which I do in the evening, and the appointments at the sunbed were, in fact, appointments with my woman, with this woman, and I think it was the same for Stephen, although I think men are able to gloss their day more easily, aren't they? . . . A screw, the shrink, a drink, can all fit under meeting. I had a meeting, there was a meeting, it was a meeting.

No, so there was no sunbed appointment, there was a therapist, and then of course, as I frantically got brown in the middle of the night I realised the half-hour under the lamp was better than anything that was going on in that terrible room in Swiss Cottage with the blasted alarm clock and the venetian blind and the joss stick or whatever it was, and the voice she had, the voice, it was like, what was it like? It was a sort of a whisper, like you'd talk to a person who was dying, a sort of whisper for the very sick and I used to boil, honestly, I felt violence towards her for this voice, and I felt violence for the silence.

I used to cry, sometimes I would go in and I would cry for
forty-five minutes, and, really, the whole forty-five minutes, and
she would sit and make sympathetic noises, sympathetic clucks,
you know, while I cried, and then the alarm clock would ring and
it would be finished, but you'd be very good, Gem, because you
have the eyes,
you have the eyes,
do you just sit here all day? what are you doing with yourself? are
you reading? what? writing? I thought of writing to you. I thought
it would be quieter. I had this theory perhaps the silence was
connected with noise, I know you're sensitive to noise, and music,
I love this ( *The music.* ) . . . is it, what is it, is it Bach? So I thought it
might just be that you wanted some peace. When my mother died
I went to Greece and just lay in the sun for two weeks and let the
sun anaesthetise me, let it just, I just lay on the sand for two weeks
and let the sun press on top of me

this is before I had the sunbed

can I smoke? I won't if, thanks, Oh God, I gave you this ashtray,
didn't I? This is the Greek experience ashtray, isn't that funny?
This is from the lying in the sand holiday, ha! It's beautiful,
isn't it?
So I can thank my mother for something, can't I? Paid for that
holiday and the car and the ashtray.

I made a list, that was one of the therapy things, my therapist
didn't ask me to do it, but I did it during that period, I made a list
of all the things I got as a result of my mother dying, what I did
with the money;
holiday
car
I had my hair streaked,
I opened an account, a sort of indulgence account.
So I had my hair streaked, and a manicure, and a facial and I
brought some silk underwear and what else? well I used most of it
for the house, I paid for the bathroom, our bathroom, which
means that every time I take a shower, I say thank you, Mum,
whenever I brush my teeth, whenever I take a pee,
thank you, Mum, and the sunbed of course,

in fact
this is our biggest bond, Stephen and I, what has kept us at least

legally as one,
the fact that we both come from suicide families.
isn't that interesting?
we were married before we found that out,

it wasn't until my mother killed herself that
I discovered his mother had too.
it was like he suddenly came out with it,
snap,
and both so cruel, really, very cruel, very cruel
his mother, he found her, his father had been dead for some,
and he went round, or went home, I think he was still a student, I
don't know all the details, anyway he found her and she had a
note pinned to her dress, and it said, 'Stephen, put the rubbish
out'.
**that was all,**
**'Stephen, put the rubbish out'.**

which was very
harsh,
I think . . .

my woman called suicide an act of homicide on the living

look at that cat!
the two of you
big cat, little cat.
purring, curled up,
it's quite unnerving, ha!
she'll never sit on my lap, will she?
I've got an incapacity to love, Gemma,
that's the
that's the
I think that's the

my ma was wearing one of my dresses
did you know that?
when she killed herself
at least she didn't leave a note
it was a summer dress and it didn't fit

it's very hard to think your way out of
something like that
to be honest

at least she finally managed to do it
she was the Sylvia Plath of South Hampstead,
my ma,
one year in ten
that's where the limp came from
known as the riding accident limp
known as the falling off the horse limp
was in fact the
throwing herself from the high building limp

she, this was when I was eleven,
she booked a room in a five-storey hotel
that was her joke when she told this nasty
little tale
I booked into a five-storey hotel in
Eastbourne,
and she
do you know I think that was the most heart
breaking thing to think that she would have been the most
beautiful woman, her face was so, I can remember before this
happened, or I think I can, but she was so twisted and, her spine
was, well you know that sort of hunch and she had to teach herself
to walk again, and what was so pathetic which is a feature of our
lives, of our deaths, isn't it? of our gestures, our grand gestures, is
that they are so human, and so trite.
She couldn't find a clear space to jump from,
she got this top room
with a balcony, but the angle or something,
there were balconies and ledges and she had to do some sort of
impossible clamber to get into a position where she could hit the
ground and then she couldn't do it, she said she hung by her
hands for
I don't know, she said an hour

and then she let go

I think she was just tired,
and of course she hit everything on the way down
apparently she didn't lose consciousness and this chap came to
her, he was one of the kitchen staff, she fell outside the kitchens,
that was her favourite part of the story
I don't know why
this chap came rushing up
and he asked her her name

and she told him a lie
she'd just jumped from this building, she'd
broken her back, her legs, her arms, her
skull, and she told him a lie
she said her name was Angela Carpenter
which was the name of the girl she'd sat next to at school.

anyway the next time she managed it
– another week and they would have converted the cooker to
North Sea Gas and that would
have been another fiasco –
I'm not sleeping with Rob any more, Gemma
We haven't for a long time, really,
I'm not sure how you found out, but I wish you hadn't
It makes something which wasn't important
become important
with me
you know, it's a thing I do
it rates with not having bra straps on my tan

this is not what I wanted to say
I wanted to say sorry
and say don't worry,

well, I wanted to say sorry

what are you thinking?
Gemma?
what are you thinking?
do you want me to go?

to tell you the absolute truth, for the past
ten minutes I've wanted to slap your face


**Gemma**'s flat. The Garden. Morning. No music.

**Gemma**  When you stop speaking, it's like stopping eating. The
first day there's something thrilling, and new, before the pain
begins. The pain where you want to give up, where you can think
of nothing else.

Then the second day, you feel wretched, the third delirious, and
then suddenly there's no appetite, it shrinks, it shrinks, until the

prospect of speaking, the thought of words retching from the mouth, how ugly and gross it seems.

Nothing changes.

How to stop people in their tracks, and make them think. Only if you're starving, if it's your son lying in your arms, or you think he might be in that discarded pile of mutilated bodies, or there's no milk in your breast and the baby's crying, or the radiation is leaking into your child's lungs, or the lead or the nitrates or the, or the, or the and all the while skirts get longer, skirts get shorter, skirts get longer, skirts get shorter, poetry is written, the news is read, I buy a different butter at the store and have my hair permed, straightened, coloured, cut, lengthened, all the while my hair keeps growing, I throw away all my skirts, a black bag to Oxfam, lately I've been at Oxfam buying back my skirts, I've stripped the pine and painted the pine, pulled out the fireplaces and put them back in, I'm on the pill, I'm off the pill, I'm on the pill, I'm off the pill. I'm listening to jazz, swing, jazz, swing, I'm getting my posters framed. I'm telling my women's group everything. I'm protesting. I'm protesting. I've covered my wall with postcards, with posters, with postcards, with posters. No this. Out them. In these. Yes those. No this. Out them. In these. Yes those. The rows. The rows with my friends, my lovers. What were they about? What did they change? The fact is, the facts are, nothing is changed. Nothing has been done. There is neither rhyme nor reason, just tears, tears, people's pain, people's rage, their aggression. And silence.

Look, already it's happening here, the weight of words, the torrent, all the words being said seep into each other, the rage, the protest all clotting together, sit and listen to the wireless and run the wheel of the tuner, spin the dial, hear them all at it, in all languages, pouring out. This is, after all, our first punishment – Babel – saying so much to say nothing. Doing so much to do nothing. Because the power to arrest, to stop us short in our tracks, what does that?

*Pause.*

but the silence, listen, how rich it is, how pregnant, how full . . .

*Pause.*

What do you remember? When all is said and done? A kiss? The taste of someone's lips? A view? A breath? A tune? The weight of your grandmother's coffin? The veins on your mother's legs. The white lines on her stomach.

Don't speak for a day and then start looking.
The senses are sharp. Look at the world about its business. The snarl. The roar. Skin stretched over the teeth. The madness.

The law is frightened of silence. It has words for the defendant who becomes mute. The wrath of God. Mute by malice. But it's not silence which is the punishment. Words. WORDS are the punishment.

The silence.

*A silence.*

beautiful
last year it was cigarettes,
the year before chocolate
but this is the best

*The Aria. 'Mache dich, Mein Hertze, Rein' from Bach's 'St Matthew Passion'. Magnificent. Released.*

# Hang Up

*for Jonathan Lunn*

**Hang Up** was first performed as a dance duet at the Sadler's Wells Theatre and first broadcast on BBC Radio 3 in November 1987. The dancers and the voices were as follows:

|  | Sadler's Wells | | Radio 3 |
| --- | --- | --- | --- |
|  | *Voices* | *Dancers* | *Voices* |
| **He** | David Threlfall | Jonathan Lunn | Anton Lesser |
| **She** | Juliet Stevenson | Lauren Potter | Juliet Stevenson |

*Choreographed by* Jonathan Lunn

*Radio broadcast directed by* Robert Cooper

*The bedroom in his house.*

*A telephone rings. It's answered.* **He** *is in the room.* **She** *is distant. We hear music at her end. Occasionally we hear Telecom line noises.*

**He** Hello.

**She** It's me.

**He** Hello.

*Pause.*

**She** It was getting late so I thought I'd call.

**He** Great.

*Pause.*

**She** Is it a bad time?

**He** No. (*Pause.*) No, no. It's a. How are you? No, it's a good time.

**She** Good. I'm fine. I'm tired. I'm fine. I'm tired. Are you, what are you doing? You weren't asleep?

**He** No. I wasn't asleep. I'm not asleep. I was, I wasn't doing anything. I'm fine. I'm great. I was just here. What are you listening to?

**She** What?

**He** The music.

**She** I don't know. It's the radio.

**He** Right. Sounds good.

**She** It's too loud, I'll turn it down.

**He** No, it's fine, I can hear you, it's nice, it gives me a sense of what, where you are, the room, the . . .

**She** You know where I am, I don't mean you, I mean me, I can't hear you properly, (*The music decreases in volume.*) that's better.

**He** It's odd, because I don't think of you as listening to music.

**She** Well, I do.

**He** Yeah.

**She** It's because we don't have the same taste.

**He** What does that mean?

**She** What I said, you don't think of me listening to music because we have different tastes, so when I've been with you, I haven't particularly wanted to listen to anything, or you know, then I feel you'll ask me what I'm listening to, or why I've tuned the radio to a particular station or, anyway, let's not have a big inquest into what music we listen to.

**He**  Have you got somebody with you or something?

**She**  No, I haven't. And that's cheap isn't it, actually, to ask that.

**He**  Is it? Why?

**She**  You know why, because it just says you don't trust me, when I'm away you don't trust me, and that's not a good feeling, it makes me feel I constantly have to defend everything I'm doing when I'm not with you, so when you ask me what sort of day I've had you're actually asking me whether I've been faithful to you. Which is not a good feeling, so that I feel you're asking me what I'm listening to in case it's a clue or something, you know: Christ!

**He**  Don't be ridiculous. I was asking you what music you were listening to because I could hear some music on and I wondered what it was and because – I just said – I miss you and you're not with me and I was trying to visualise where you were, what you were doing, what you looked like, and the room, and what you were listening to, it's got nothing to do with clues . . .

**She**  Except you say is there anyone in the room with me, and I feel you're creating this thing, because you can be really paranoid, honestly, and I can just see you thinking: you see! She's in the room with somebody and she's listening to music and everything and before I know it I'm having an affair. So please. Just. You know.

**He**  I'm sorry. Okay. I'm sorry. Christ, I hate this, I hate not being able to, everything becomes out of, I mean, Christ, I'm just asking about a piece of music, I wish I'd never bothered now, because. . . (*Sighing.*)

**She**  Right. Listen, are you going to call me back? Because if we're going to talk more, you'd better call me, because it's not my house and –

**He**  Right.

**She**  What?

**He**  Right, I'll call you back.

**She**  If you'd rather not . . .

**He** Of course I want to call you back, come on!

**She** Okay.

**He** I'll put the phone down.

**She** Right.

**He** I'm putting it down. 'Bye.

*Phone down. Rapid fade out.*

*Fade up on her hallway – we hear the same music coming from another room. Phone rings and is picked up immediately by her.* **She** *is in hallway.* **He** *is now distant.*

**She** Hello.

**He** It's me.

**She** So . . .

**He** This is a better line.

**She** Yes.

**He** I'm missing you.

**She** Thank you.

**He** Don't say thank you. Say you're missing me.

**She** I'm missing you.

**He** Are you?

**She** I'm going to have to borrow a fire tonight, I think, or something, because it's so cold in this room – the radiator's supposed to be on, but it's freezing – so yes, I'm missing not being at home. Yes. Okay?

**He** Which home? My home? Your home?

**She** Both. They're both warmer than this place.

**He** Okay.

**She** My bed at home doesn't have you in it, so your bed would be best.

**He** My electric blanket.

**She** And your electric blanket.

**He** And my radiators.

**She** And your radiators. *My* hot-water bottle.

**He**  *My* carpet in the bathroom.

**She**  Your carpet in the bathroom.

**He**  I'm missing you.

**She**  Did you go out tonight, or what?

**He**  No. I hadn't called, because, no I did go out briefly, I was out earlier for a while, but I was going to call you late because I wanted to have this conversation last thing, you know: go to sleep with your voice still uh. What's the bed like?

**She**  Okay. It's okay. It's not great. It sags a bit. It sags a bit. It's okay.

**He**  Were you planning on coming back at the weekend, or what?

**She**  I don't know yet. I don't know. I'll see. Maybe. Why?

**He**  No, it's just that if you weren't, if you can't, maybe I could come over, if that's a good idea, I'll come over there and you know: sag in your bed.

**She**  Okay. Obviously, if I have to work on Saturday, it wouldn't be, I don't think there'd be much point, would there? it would be a long way to come for one day, but if I'm not, I've got a feeling we will though, because that's always the way, isn't it?

**He**  Right. Sure.

**She**  The one weekend you'd like off.

**He**  That's right.

**She**  What's your week like?

**He**  Fine. Fine. You know. Fine. I don't know. Yes.

**She**  Have you seen anybody?

**He**  No. Not really. I've seen a few people. At work, obviously. I've had lunch and things. But not, no, not really, no, just pottered about.

**She**  So what was it this evening?

**He**  What?

**She**  Where were you when I was waiting for you to call me?

**He**  Were you waiting for me to call you? I was going to call you at eleven, I was just thinking that and then the telephone rang.

**She**  No, well I was going to go to bed and I thought I'll get into bed and then the phone will ring, because it's out in the hall and otherwise I'm standing in a t-shirt in the hall and it's really public, me and the bicycles and the hall and – in fact – I wear your dufflecoat. I'm using it as a dressing-gown. I wear your dufflecoat to the loo. So I thought I'd ring before all that, because otherwise people come back and there I am.

**He**  That's nice. I like the thought of you wearing my dufflecoat. No, I saw my friend, Susie.

**She**  What?

**He**  This evening, I saw my friend, Susie. We had a drink. It wasn't arranged. I bumped into her, so we had a drink, a quick drink.

**She**  Why do you do that? Say that? 'My friend' like that? You don't have to say that.

**He**  What do you mean?

**She**  You know what I mean, calling her *my friend* as if that, as if by saying that it doesn't count or something, because you can just say you had a drink with Susie and that's fine.

**He**  Okay, I had a drink with Susie.

**She**  Fine.

**He**  Who's my friend, you know.

**She**  No, you wouldn't say, I was having a drink with my friend David, would you?

**He**  I might, I might, I don't know, and anyway I don't live with a man, if I lived with a man I might feel the need to distinguish between friends and anything else, not that I live with you, but you get the gist, I don't know, this was what I was saying earlier to my non-friend, friend, Susie as it happens, that a lot of this has got to do with not actually doing it, not actually being able to make a commitment, because everything then gets so complicated because obviously you need to look at your place and then you're away, or I'm away and there just aren't enough days of normality, **of just simple days without, there's nothing simple, I can't remember what I was going to say now, what was I saying?** To do with having both flats. I can't think, well it just means nothing feels firm, so I don't relax and then I end up sounding like I'm worried there's someone in the room with you, which I am – I suppose, in my heart of hearts, I do – and so much time just spent talking without seeing you and not laughing, not doing things together and . . . this is not what I was trying to say, I had a really clear sense of it when I was talking, earlier, it's hopeless, and I'm still wondering, whether you're alone. I wanted to go over to your flat and ransack it, I didn't want to, but sometimes, I get very wound up and then I want to go over and just ransack the place from top to bottom.

**She** Have you? I hope you're joking, because if –

**He** (*interrupting*) I said, I haven't but sometimes –

**She** (*interrupting*) I promise you, if I thought you'd gone over to the flat when I wasn't there, I couldn't forgive you, Christ, I feel so stifled sometimes.

**He** I said, I haven't been over to your flat. I said I sometimes get the urge to. I haven't been to your flat. I haven't been anywhere near it.

**She** Anyway. I feel very tense about that. I feel very strongly about it. I think you should give me back the key.

**He** Okay. I didn't ask you for the key. You gave me the key so I could check the mail and the answerphone, but I'm very happy to give you the key back.

**She** And I'm aware of what you're trying to say, what you were saying earlier, about things being complicated, they are, but that's a choice we've made, isn't it? And we both agreed and like everything sometimes it works and sometimes it doesn't, but it means we're not possessions, we're not taking each other for granted, we're not the carpet in the bathroom.

**He** Sometimes I'd like to be the carpet in the bathroom.

**She** Sometimes you are. Sometimes I am.

**He** Yeah. I know. I know. Do you know, this morning on the tube, I got an early tube and it was, it wasn't crowded or anything, and the lights didn't work properly, they kept fading out, and we kept stopping for signals, but anyway, the point is opposite me, on the other seats, there was this couple and they were both, they were thing, mildly sub, handicapped, obviously not severe, they looked ordinary enough, but they were reading comics, children's comics and . . . the *Beezer*, you know . . . *Bunty* . . . and, anyway, as it started stopping and the lights are coming on and off every five minutes and I realised what they're doing, they're starting to giggle, and what's happening is, every time the lights go off they're kissing, just kissing and then springing apart as the lights come on, so the lights would go off, then come on, and there'd be this flurry of activity and then they'd spring apart and read their comics with these huge grins, because they'd been kissing, and I just thought, Oh God, I miss you and I love you and where are you? So, I guess, well I'm sad today, that's all. It was so tender. And I just . . . (*Sighs.*) Are you still there?

**She** Yes.

**He** I don't know what I'm talking about.

**She** There is someone here.

**He** Right.

**She** I didn't see the point in telling you. There seemed no point. It's just hurtful.

**He** Right.

**She** Because it's nothing. You see, Christ (*Sighs.*) it's nothing. It's nothing, for either of us, for him either, but now it's something. And I didn't mean it to be. It's nothing.

**He** So you rang me so I wouldn't disturb you.

**She** I can't say anything. Whatever I say now. How can I say anything?

**He** I knew anyway.

**She** What? What did you know?

**He** I knew you were with somebody.

**She** How?

**He** I went to your flat.

**She** I don't believe you.

**He** That's why I saw Susie. I had to speak to somebody. I went to the flat and then I called Susie. I had to tell somebody. So. I told Susie.

**She** Is Susie there now?

**He** No.

*She sighs.*

**He** I should go.

**She** (*suddenly loud*) Please, would you turn that off. (*Pause.*) I'm talking to you.

*The music is turned off.*

Thank you.

**He**  What?

**She**  I was asking for the radio to be turned off, I can't think, I can't cope with the music. I wasn't talking to you.

**He**  I'm going.

**She**  I'm sitting on a bicycle.

**He**  What?

**She**  I'm sitting on a bicycle. Someone's bike in the hall.Listen. (*A cycle bell rings.*) That's the bell. I could just peddle off in my t-shirt and dufflecoat.

**He**  In my dufflecoat.

**She**  Yeah.

**He**  Peddle down to me.

**She**  Shall I?

**He**  Yeah, please.

*Pause.*

**She**  It's very quiet now. Which phone are you on? Upstairs?

**He**  Yes.

*Pause.*

**She**  Don't hang up.

*Pause.*

I've only ever known one mentally handicapped person. This was years ago. He was my age, and sweet, really very sweet, and he had a girlfriend and she was deaf and dumb. Nobody could understand her, honestly, nobody, she wouldn't sign or anything, the sign language: she wouldn't, but this guy doted on her, he had the kind of personality would be patient with anybody. He'd push an old person around in a wheelchair all day if they wanted, real patience, and with children, and he was the same with this deaf and dumb girl and the way he understood her, the way they got on together was he talked for them both, so like he'd ask her a question and then do the answer for her: 'Want a cup of tea?' 'Yes please.' 'Do you want sugar?' 'Yes please, two please.' 'Cup of tea, two sugars, coming up,' and that's how they got on together, it was perfect. (*Back to the present.*) It's nothing. I would have told you, probably. I don't know. I wouldn't have told you. There's nothing to tell. I'd like to cycle down to you now. Darling?

*Pause.*

Darling? Are you still there?

**He** *sighs.*

'Yes, I'm still here.' 'Good, I thought you'd gone for a minute.' 'No, still here.' 'Good, because I wanted to tell you I'm missing you too.' 'Thank you.' 'And we'll be all right, I'll cycle down to you, in my t-shirt and my dufflecoat, all night and we'll be fine.' (*The cycle bell rings again.*)

*He puts down the receiver.*

**She** (*normal voice*) Johnny? Johnny? (*Beat.*) Johnny?

*Silence.*

# What If It's Raining?

*For Hannah and all those to whom we ran for cover*

'If I loved you, they said, I'd leave
and find my own affairs.
Well, once again this April, we've
come round to the bears;

punished and cared for, behind bars,
the coons on bread and water
stretch thin black fingers after ours.
And you are still my daughter.'

*Heart's Needle, W.D. Snodgrass*

**What If It's Raining?** was a Limehouse production, first shown on Channel 4 in 1986, with the following cast:

| | |
|---|---|
| **Dominic** | Michael Maloney |
| **Marilyn** | Deborah Findlay |
| **Philip** | Miles Anderson |
| **Jack** | Jack Bentall |
| **Joseph** | Bernard Paddon |
| **Siobhan** | Eve Matheson |
| **Chris** | Chris Jury |
| **Angie** | Kamilla Blanche |
| **Stephanie** | Jane Gurnett |

*Director* Stephen Whittaker
*Producer* Mark Shivas

# Part One

**Dominic/Marilyn**'s house. Thursday. Early evening.

**Dominic** is in his study. His son **Jack** in one arm, drawing with the other. He is a cartoonist. He draws on huge pieces of paper. The one he's working on now has the sheet divided into four boxes.

1. A baby crying in a father's arms.
2. Father trying to amuse the baby.
3. Father frantic to amuse the baby. Toys, noises, funny faces.
The baby bawls.
4. Father asleep. Baby bawls.

**Dominic** adds the caption: 'Getting Baby off to Sleep'. The cartoon completed, he turns his attention to **Jack**. **Jack** has been patiently sucking on anything within reach, but he needs getting off to sleep himself.

**Dominic** (to **Jack**)  Where's Mum, eh?

Mum – **Marilyn** – is late. **Dominic** wants to go to a launch party for a book he has illustrated, but he cannot go out until she gets back. He puts lids on pens, stands and carries **Jack** through to his bedroom. He lays the baby in his cot. **Jack** is quiet. **Dominic** stands by the door for a second, then dims the light and makes to go. **Jack** cries.

**Dominic** (coming straight back in)  Not going to go to sleep, eh?

He picks up the baby and they go downstairs to the kitchen/dining room. **Dominic** puts **Jack** in his high chair, and quickly prepares him a bowl of cereal. The television is on, flickering. A string quartet bleeds through from the stereo.

**Dominic**  Now listen, rat face, scoff this muck, okay, and get tired! And I won't listen to any more excuses. Asleep in five minutes or bum severely bitten. (**Jack** cries.) Hey, I was joking. I'm sorry darling.

**Philip**'s flat. The same time.

**Philip** owns a shop which sells paintings, antiques and beautiful things. Upstairs is his flat. This is equally tasteful; indeed many of the things here are part of the population which is for sale.

**Marilyn** is here, wearing only a shirt. She begins getting herself together to leave.

**Marilyn**  I'm so late.

**Philip**  You could say the exhibition held you up. You wanted to discuss rehanging stuff or whatever.

**Marilyn**  I mean for the baby.

**Philip**  He'll be asleep.

**Marilyn**  No. Well, maybe.

**Philip**  How is Dominic with him? He dotes on him, doesn't he?

**Marilyn**  He dotes on his photographs. He's fine with him. Yes.

**Philip**  But?

**Marilyn**  I feel as if I've spent the entire evening criticising him. (*Pause.*) He undoes everything I do. I don't think he means to.

**Philip**  What are you doing? (**Marilyn** *is scrabbling around by the couch. She finds her knickers and holds them up to him.*) Oh right.

**Marilyn**  (*dressing*) I do love him. That's the point. And I come here to see you, to talk, to be myself a bit, and . . . (*She's trying to excuse the affair.*)

**Philip**  What?

**Marilyn**  Making love. It's getting to be a habit. How did it start?

**Philip**  When you go to see people, to talk, do you always take your diaphragm with you?

**Marilyn**  That's not fair, Philip.

**Philip**  Well let's start off being honest, shall we? And see how long it lasts.


**Dominic/Marilyn**'s *bedroom. A little later.*

**Dominic** *is dressing for a smart function. Clothes on the bed, everywhere. He's late. He pauses as he hears* **Marilyn** *coming in, the doors quietly thudding as first she checks downstairs, taking in the mess, the television droning, the lights left on, then comes upstairs to check on* **Jack**. *She comes into their bedroom.*

**Marilyn**  Sorry. When did he go off?

**Dominic**  Early. Then he woke up.

**Marilyn**  Why?

**Dominic**  I've no idea.

**Marilyn**  How come all the rooms downstairs have everything turned on?

**Dominic**  What everything?

**Marilyn**  The TV. Everything.

**Dominic**  I'm actually very late.

**Marilyn**  I know. I said sorry. The gallery, the exhibition, there were things to sort out.

**Dominic**  Right. How's Philip?

**Marilyn**  He's fine. You know.

**Dominic**  (*putting on his shoes*)  Look, I owe him a pound. Will you give it to him? And I think Jack's getting more teeth or something. His bottom's sore again.

**Marilyn**  Did you change him before he went off?

**Dominic**  Yes.

**Marilyn**  You have to put loads of that cream on because he wets himself and it gets rinsed off . . .

**Dominic**  (*interrupting her*)  I know. I did that.

**Marilyn** *realises she is being over-anxious. A pause.*

**Dominic**  Look, uh, I'm probably going to get landed with bringing some of the people back. It's the form. So bear with me, eh? It'll be late. We'll probably have to eat first. (*Pause.*) And I'm not sure where Joseph's going to stay the night.

**Marilyn**  Why do you have to say it like that? Probably this, probably that. You know full well you will eat, and they will come back, and Joseph will stay here. Why not just say that?

**Dominic**  Because that's how you respond. Why don't you come? I'm sure Pippa would uh . . .

**Marilyn**  Why ask now?

**Dominic**  It's the first book I've illustrated. It's important to me. I don't want to have to ask you. Anyway I'll see you Marilyn.

*He is about to leave, but* **Marilyn** *speaks.* **Dominic** *stands framed by the door.*

**Marilyn**  Is it just tonight?

**Dominic**  No. Tonight's the university thing. Tomorrow night's the publishers. I told you.

**Marilyn** You didn't, actually. And it's not in the diary. (*Pause. Softening.*) Good luck.

**Dominic** Thanks.

**Marilyn** (*gently*) And I hope nobody likes the book and you get dysentery from the curry.

**Dominic** Lasagne.

**Marilyn** I'll try to come tomorrow, okay?

**Dominic** *nods. He exits.* **Marilyn** *surveys the wreckage of the bedroom.*

**Dominic/Marilyn**'s *house. A few hours later.*

**Marilyn** *opens the front door to* **Philip**.

**Philip** Bad time?

**Marilyn** *is surprised. Before she can answer,* **Philip** *assumes 'yes'.*

**Philip** Right.

**Marilyn** (*stopping him before he leaves*) Good time. Come in.

**Philip** *comes in. He is wearing a cap.*

**Philip** I came disguised. How did you recognise me?

**Marilyn** (*flustered*) Do you want a drink or something?

**Philip** Hey, I'm not staying, don't panic. I was just passing.

**Marilyn** Where are you going?

**Philip** Home.

**Marilyn** Where've you come from?

**Philip** Home. This is directly on my way back. I have a voucher which says you owe me one kiss. (*He produces a small piece of paper.*) Is this your signature?

*In spite of herself, she laughs. She gives him a polite kiss, then pulls his cap down over his eyes.*

I missed you.

**Marilyn** I've only been gone a few hours.

**Philip** I've been missing you a few hours.

**Marilyn** Safe journey.

*She opens the door and gently pushes him out.*


**Dominic/Marilyn**'s *house. The same day. Late.*

*The front door opens and* **Dominic**, **Joseph** *and* **Siobhan** *come in unloading coats, high-spirited.* **Joseph** *is small, bespectacled. Rather serious, rather feeble. He wrote the book which* **Dominic** *has illustrated.* **Siobhan** *is a postgraduate and President of the University Literary Society. She has organised the evening.*

**Dominic** Sssh! Keep it down because Jack's asleep.

*They go into the kitchen.* **Dominic** *turns on the light.*

I'll just report in. Then I'll pop the kettle on. No, I'll pop the kettle on then I'll report in. Or would you rather have a scotch Joseph? Siobhan? Tea? Coffee?

**Siobhan** I'll have the scotch, if that's okay?

**Dominic** Yes, of course it's okay. (*Changes his mind again.*) Listen I'll just say hello upstairs. Then I'll sort you out.

**Joseph** Thank you.

**Dominic** (*exiting*) Excuse me.

**Siobhan** (*to* **Joseph**, *smiling*) I'll put the kettle on.


**Dominic/Marilyn**'s *bedroom. Dark.*

**Dominic** (*at the door*) Darling?

**Marilyn** *is asleep. He moves to the bed, switches on the table lamp, and nuzzles up to her.*

**Dominic** Darling?

**Marilyn** Ngh?

**Dominic** Sorry it's so late. You okay?

**Marilyn** Ngh.

**Dominic** Listen, I've said it's all right if we put Joseph up.

**Marilyn** Uh-huh.

**Dominic**  Did Jack wake up? Oh and some people have come back for a coffee.

**Marilyn**  Did you have to wake me up to tell me these things?

**Dominic**  I just wanted to check about Joseph.

**Marilyn**  What if I'd said no?

**Dominic**  I think it was a success.

**Marilyn**  What was?

**Dominic**  This evening.

**Marilyn**  Uh-huh.

**Dominic**  And we did have curry. And Joseph's threatening dysentery. (*He laughs into the duvet.*)

**Marilyn**  Right.

**Dominic**  Right, well I'll see you in a sec, then. I'll just run Siobhan home and come back to bed.

**Marilyn**  Why can't she get a cab?

**Dominic**  It's all right. I won't wake you. And if the baby does, I'll see to him.

**Marilyn**  (*disbelieving*)  Yeah.

**Dominic**  (*kissing her*)  Night, night, cynic. You smell nice.

**Marilyn**  You smell of tandoori.

**Dominic**  (*correcting her*)  Sag Gosht.

**Marilyn**  Same to you.

**Dominic** *exits. He's left the light on.* **Marilyn** *leans over to turn it off.*


**Dominic** *driving* **Siobhan** *home.*

*VW Beetle pops along the streets.* **Siobhan** *is very keen on* **Dominic**.

**Siobhan**  I like the book, Dominic. Very much.

**Dominic**  Thanks.

**Siobhan**  Fantastic drawings. Beautiful.

**Dominic**  Oh, I think the text is the thing. Joseph's extraordinary.

*They arrive.*

**Siobhan** Thanks for driving me home. I could easily have walked.

**Dominic** No trouble. Um, how's your research?

**Siobhan** Oh, slow. Lot of time asking myself why I'm doing it. A lot of time doing other things. Like tonight.

**Dominic** Hey, yes, thanks for tonight. I'm sorry I'm not better at it. When two or three people are gathered together I'm a disaster.

**Siobhan** (*genuinely*) I don't think so. By the way, I'm happy to baby-sit tomorrow. I mean not only for your squash, but the whole evening if Marilyn would like to go to the do with you.

**Dominic** Thanks very much. I might take you up on that. she's got an exhibition for Oxfam. But um . . . Anyway.

**Siobhan** The way you and Marilyn live restores my faith in the institution. Because you lead your own lives, give each other space.

**Dominic** You lower your expectations. That's how things work. I sometimes think that's what maturity is. Lowering your expectations.

**Siobhan** Have you ever been attracted to anyone else?

**Dominic** (*a little manipulative*) Uh, have I ever been attracted to anyone else? Well you see I mean, the clever thing about marriage and kids and things is that it sort of guarantees you're just too busy surviving really, to do anything about it. Even if you were.

**Siobhan** (*feeling in her pockets*) I hope I've got my key . . . Yes.

**Dominic** Thanks for . . .

**Siobhan** Thank you.

*They embrace briefly. A polite kiss.*

**Dominic** (*as she gets out*) You all right there?

**Siobhan** Yes.

**Dominic** Sleep tight.

*He relaxes back into his seat, turns on the car stereo, pleased with himself, then drives off.*

**Dominic/Marilyn**'s *bedroom. A little later.*

**Dominic** *is fast asleep.* **Marilyn** *enters, carrying a wide-awake* **Jack**. *She gets into bed, putting baby between herself and* **Dominic**. *She whispers to* **Jack**: *sleep would be in order.* **Jack** *is not persuaded. He begins to wail.* **Dominic** *is fast asleep.*

**Dominic/Marilyn**'s *house. Kitchen/dining room. The following morning.*

**Marilyn** *enters, late: she has to take* **Jack** *to* **Hilary**'s. *She is well-dressed despite the rush.* **Joseph** *is at the fridge, visibly embarrassed at being found holding a carton of milk.* **Marilyn** *has probably only met* **Joseph** *once or twice before. She moves quickly around the kitchen, preparing a lightning breakfast. She has* **Jack** *under one arm as she does so. She's very capable.*

**Joseph**  Ah. Hello. I'm just making –

**Marilyn**  Go ahead.

**Joseph**  Is it all right if I use this milk?

**Marilyn**  Help yourself.

**Joseph**  Dominic did tell –

**Marilyn**  You're welcome to stay. I'm sorry, I'm late. I'm sure when Dominic gets down he'll tell you where everything is . . .

**Joseph**  Oh, I don't need, I can . . . as long as I'm not.

**Marilyn** *isn't paying a great deal of attention.* **Joseph** *retreats to cereal and a book.* **Marilyn** *puts* **Jack** *in his chair and ties a pink bib round his neck.*

**Marilyn**  Incidentally, this is the brat. Jack, this is Joseph.

**Joseph**  It's a he, yes?

**Marilyn**  It is. (*Deadpan.*) Hence the pink.

**Joseph**  I'm afraid I don't know much about children.

**Marilyn**  Nor do I.

**Joseph**  (*disbelieving*) Oh . . .

**Marilyn**  No, really. By the way, I love the book. It's marvellous.

**Joseph**  Thank you. That's the nearest I've got to childbirth.

**Marilyn** What is?

**Joseph** Writing the book. I felt as though I were giving birth.

**Marilyn** (*unimpressed*) Why was that?

*She does not require a reply, but* **Joseph** *offers one nonetheless. It is lost, because* **Marilyn** *is talking to* **Jack**.

**Marilyn** Now look, are you going to eat something instant or do we have to hang around for boiled egg? Egg, huh? Okay, I'll join you.

*As* **Marilyn** *busies herself with the eggs,* **Dominic** *enters.*

**Dominic** Hey, why didn't you wake me?

**Marilyn** (*genuine*) You were tired. You were asleep. (*She hands him a mug ot tea.*)

**Dominic** Thank you. Morning Joseph. How did you sleep?

**Joseph** Well. Fine.

**Dominic** *ignores him as* **Marilyn** *did; he goes to* **Jack**.

**Dominic** (*cooing to* **Jack**) Hello! (*To* **Marilyn**.) Darling. I'll take Jack to Hilary's. You'll be late.

**Marilyn** No, I need the car. I'm going back to the exhibition.

**Joseph** What's this?

**Marilyn** It's an exhibition I'm organising for a local gallery, for Oxfam. It's by Chilean refugees. It's mostly wall-hangings. You should come and see.

**Dominic** If you see Philip remind him we're playing squash at six o'clock.

**Marilyn** You're playing squash with Philip?

**Dominic** I told you. And that girl – thing, the Literary Society girl . . . Siobhan. She said she'd sit for us the whole evening. If you do want to come with me to the jamboree.

**Marilyn** I don't know. I'm not playing squash, anyway. Liz is away.

**Dominic** Well come and play with Philip and me. We can swap round.

**Marilyn** I don't know. (*To* **Jack**.) Are you going to have blackcurrant?

**Dominic** I'll feed him, darling, and you can get ready.

**Marilyn** Or I can feed me.

**Dominic** Or I could feed you and he could get ready. (*They laugh.* **Dominic** *looks to* **Jack***. Puts on his cooing voice.*) Hey! He slept through! No wonder we're all so jolly! (*To* **Joseph***.*) Sorry about this, Joseph: blissful family life.

*Squash Court. The same day, 7pm.*

*A squash ball slams into the wall.* **Dominic** *is playing* **Philip***.* **Dominic** *is having to do more of the running.*

*Through the glass back wall of the court,* **Marilyn** *watches* **Dominic** *lose the game. She is dressed for squash herself.* **Dominic** *loses, huffs, puffs. Then he turns and speaks through the glass to* **Marilyn***.*

**Dominic** Come in and rescue me.

**Marilyn** No, you carry on.

**Dominic** No, no, no: I've lulled him into a false sense of security. You'll demolish him now. (*He comes heaving out of the court.*) 'Specially in those shorts.

**Marilyn** Shut up.

**Dominic** (*holding the door for her to go in*) Take my advice. Cheat. (*Kisses her.*) I'll go and ring Siobhan and see if Jack's okay.

**Marilyn** Great.

**Dominic** Philip, cheers. Thanks very much.

**Dominic** *exits.*

**Philip** Play for service?

*He hits the ball onto the wall. They play silently.* **Marilyn** *misses. She picks up the ball, serves, begins to cry. They play for a few seconds.* **Marilyn** *sinks to the floor and sobs.*

**Marilyn** God, Philip. What are we doing? What am I doing? What am I playing at?

**Philip** *kneels and comforts her.*

**Philip** Come on, let's play.

**Marilyn** I can't.

**Philip** What are you doing after this?

**Marilyn** There's a promotional thing for Dominic and Joseph's book. I'm supposed to be going.

**Philip** Spend the evening with me.

**Marilyn** I can't.

*They get up.*

**Philip** I'll take you home.

**Marilyn** We've got a sitter.

**Philip** I'll take her home. Then I'll come back.

**Marilyn** Philip, I can't.

**Philip** You can do anything you want. If you don't want to, don't.

**Dominic** *appears at the court door.*

**Dominic** Who's winning?

**Philip** Oh it's uh . . . pretty even.

**Dominic** Well hurry up and finish. I want to –

**Marilyn** Dom, I'm feeling a bit sick. (*Aside to* **Philip**.) I do actually feel as if I could throw up.

**Dominic** (*coming into the court, concerned*) Hey, are you okay?

**Marilyn** Yeah.

**Dominic** Well look, you've probably overdone it a bit. Let's get you sat down.

**Marilyn** I think I'll get changed.

**Dominic** Okay.

**Marilyn** Philip said he'll take me home.

**Philip** No problem.

**Dominic** (*deflated*) Oh . . . it's just that –

**Marilyn** I know. Your promotion thing. It's just that I feel a bit sick.

**Dominic** Look, if you're worried about the baby, Siobhan said he's fast asleep.

**Marilyn** It's not the baby. I just don't feel up to –

**Philip** It really is no problem to take her home.

*A beat.* **Dominic** *is not happy.*

**Dominic** Right.


**Marilyn/Dominic**'s *bedroom. Later that evening.*

**Marilyn** *and* **Philip** *are naked on the bed. Intent, holding each other.* **Marilyn** *suddenly disengages.*

**Marilyn** (*explaining*) Jack.

*Now we hear a sob.*

**Philip** What?

**Marilyn** He's woken up. Sorry. (*Quickly gets out of bed and grabs her dressing-gown.*)

**Philip** Do you always go straight to him?

**Marilyn** Yes.

**Philip** Doesn't he ever go back to sleep by himself?

**Marilyn** No.

**Marilyn** *goes through to* **Jack**'s *bedroom. She picks him up and starts trying to pat him off to sleep.* **Philip** *comes in, dressing himself at the same time. He comes up behind* **Marilyn** *and puts his arm around her and the baby.*

**Philip** I love you. I'd love you both.

**Marilyn** If we ever came to you, he'd break all your beautiful things.

**Jack** *miraculously settles down.* **Philip** *and* **Marilyn** *smile. The world full of sign and portent.*


**Dominic/Marilyn**'s *bedroom. Later.*

**Marilyn** *is asleep in bed.* **Dominic** *gets in.*

**Dominic** Hi. You feel nice.

**Marilyn** (*hazily*) What time is it?

**Dominic** Dunno.

**Marilyn**  Have you been drinking?

**Dominic**  Yeah. (*He moves up against her in the bed.*)

**Marilyn**  Dom, I really need to sleep.

**Dominic**  Then why did you put your cap in?

**Marilyn** (*waking up fast*)  What?

**Dominic**  I am a private detective. I snooped in your bathroom, and could not find the object in question. I submit, madam. Have your evil way with me.

**Marilyn**  Are you doing this deliberately, Dominic?

**Dominic**  Doing what?

**Marilyn**  Because if you are, it's sick, that's all.

**Dominic** (*deflated*)  What's sick? That I want to make love with you?

**Marilyn**  Oh Christ. (*She sits up.*) I think we should talk.

**Dominic**  I don't want to talk. I'm drunk. I want to make love with you.

**Marilyn**  Great.

**Dominic**  Well it may not be great, Marilyn, but it's what I feel.

**Marilyn**  And I feel we should talk or sleep.

**Dominic**  Yeah. Okay.

*Abruptly, he rolls over to go to sleep. Long pause.*

I'm trying to count sheep. And they've all got erections.

*Busy Park. The following afternoon.*

**Marilyn** and **Philip** *are walking, pushing a sleeping* **Jack**.

**Marilyn**  Do you need to get back?

**Philip**  Probably.

**Marilyn**  Thanks for coming with us.

**Philip**  Will Dom be at home?

**Marilyn**  Yes. He's working. He's got a cartoon to finish and it's late.

**Philip** I'm glad.

**Marilyn** Why's that?

**Philip** Otherwise I couldn't have seen you.

**Marilyn** Oh, we never do this, Philip. That's not how we work. Our day is inched out into schedules and permutations: Dom/Jack, Marilyn/Jack, Dom work/Marilyn work. Dom out/Marilyn in, Marilyn out/Dom in. And so on. And so forth.

**Philip** Why?

**Marilyn** Why? Well because of who we are. What we want. Because of him. And because of me. (*Pause.*) Anyway I'm going to have to say something about us.

**Dominic/Marilyn**'s *house: kitchen/dining room. The same day. Late afternoon.*

**Marilyn** *comes in to find* **Joseph** *at the table, eating and reading: feed the brain. Elsewhere on the table there is evidence of shopping in quantity: wine, pasta.*

**Marilyn** Hi.

**Joseph** Hello.

**Marilyn** What's all this?

**Joseph** (*guilty*) Oh. I was just feeling a bit peckish. Hope you don't –

**Marilyn** No. I mean the shopping.

**Joseph** Dominic got it for tonight.

**Marilyn** For what tonight?

**Joseph** Well, at the thing last night, he invited Christopher and the chap from Penguin – well, anyway, it's four, I think. Plus you and Dominic.

**Marilyn** Right.

**Marilyn** *goes to the table in the hall and checks the diary. She goes upstairs to tackle* **Dominic**.

**Dominic** *is in his study, working on his cartoon strip. This one shows a sleepless man in bed counting sheep. The sheep have erections.* **Marilyn** *comes in.* **Dominic** *doesn't look round, but continues drawing. His stereo* *is playing. As they talk he rejects ideas and screws up quantities of paper.*

**Dominic** (*of the mess*) I know, sorry. It's a tip.

**Marilyn** Why do you do this? (*The cartoon, the sheep.*) It used to be funny. It's not funny any more.

**Dominic** Oh, I never find it funny.

**Marilyn** You do this instead of talking.

**Dominic** No, I do it instead of fucking, actually. Speaking of the second to last time we did that, where's Jack?

**Marilyn** He's downstairs. He's asleep in the hall. I wanted to talk tonight. I didn't want to have people round here for dinner.

**Dominic** You're very keen on this talk all of a sudden. (*He is still drawing frantically.*)

**Marilyn** Will you look at me?

*He slowly takes off his glasses, switches off the music with his remote control, then turns at last to face her.*

**Dominic** I'm not joking when I say I have to finish this. I have to get it round to them this evening. I'm sorry. It's my work. It's not Oxfam. It's not deserving. It probably is a complete confection, but it's what I do and I get paid for it. Inviting publishers round is part of the business. (*He puts his glasses back on and starts working again.*)

**Marilyn** I'm very unhappy, Dominic.

**Dominic** Well right. That's why you want to talk. You've yet to come in here and say 'I'm happy: I want to talk.'

**Marilyn** Are you happy with me being like this?

**Dominic** I love you.

**Marilyn** Dominic, darling. That's not what I asked. Anyway, what's the point? When I do say anything it only ends up in one of your pictures.

**Dominic** (*drawing frantically*) I'm trying to remember the last time you called me darling.

**Marilyn** (*angry, frustrated*) Dominic, please. (*She turns to leave.*)

**Dominic** The Chinese, on the other hand – did you know this? – the Chinese have no word for darling –

**Dominic** *is cut off by the sound of the door slamming behind* **Marilyn***. He* *looks round at the closed door, then clicks on the music and returns to work.*

**Dominic/Marilyn** *'s house: downstairs. That evening.*

**Marilyn** *is sat at the table. It is laid for the dinner party. There is pasta on the stove.* **Marilyn** *simmers along with the sauce.* **Dominic** *bounces in through the front door.*

**Dominic** (*calling*) Darling! (*Comes into the kitchen/dining area. Sees the food. Sees* **Marilyn**.) Hi. Smells good.

**Marilyn** I thought you said you'd be back at 7.30.

**Dominic** Oh, Alan was there and some people it was important to meet. What should I do? (*He means the food.*)

**Marilyn** It's done.

**Dominic** Oh. (*Excited.*) Hey, it went really well. Oh, and I've got a thing in *Harpers*! Good, eh?

**Marilyn** Tremendous. Dominic –

**Dominic** (*not listening*) Where's Jack? Is he asleep?

**Marilyn** I think so. Dominic –

**Dominic** (*not listening*) Thanks for doing this, darling. (*He means the food, which he stirs and tastes.*) Must have taken you ages. Did you use a stock cube?

**Marilyn** I'm going up to my parents' tonight. (**Dominic** *turns, concerned.*)

**Dominic** Why? What? Is somebody ill? What, Marilyn?

**Marilyn** I need some time on my own. To think.

**Dominic** Oh, what, is the baby getting on top of you? (*Decides that's what it is.*) Yeah, me too. I know. (*Planning.*) All right. I'll drive you up first thing in the morning. Actually – no I can't, uh –

**Marilyn** I want to take the baby with me. And Philip said he'd drive us.

**Dominic** Why Philip?

**Marilyn** Because I think I'm in love with him. (*Pause.*) I've been trying to tell you.

*A long pause.* **Dominic** *stirs the sauce, not looking at her.*

**Dominic** This 'love'. (*He makes the word sound unpleasant.*) It's a mutual love, is it?

**Marilyn** Yes.

**Dominic** (*still stirring*) You screwing him, are you? (**Marilyn** *does not reply.*) In our bed?

**Marilyn** Dominic . . . don't.

**Dominic** I want to know if you've been fucking in our bed?

**Marilyn** Yes, we have.

**Dominic** Right. How many times? (*No reply.*) What are you pausing for? You counting?

**Marilyn** Don't do this, Dominic. Please.

**Dominic** Philip? Oh Christ. (*Pause. Turns to her, sudden realisation.*) Of course! Your cap!

*The doorbell rings.* **Marilyn** *gets up quickly.*

**Marilyn** That'll be Philip. He thought he ought to come round, so we could talk.

*Pause.*

**Dominic** Oh yeah. Let's have Phil in for a chat.

**Marilyn** Shall I go? If you don't want to see hin. I'll ask him to wait in the car. (*The bell rings again.*) Well?

**Dominic** Let Philip in, Marilyn.

**Marilyn** *goes out to the hall. Sound of voices. She reappears with* **Joseph**.

**Marilyn** It's Joseph.

**Dominic** Hello Joseph. Silly: we thought you were Marilyn's lover. (**Joseph** *is dumbfounded. He grins inanely. The doorbell rings again.*) Oh no – that'll be him now. I'll go.

**Dominic** *opens the front door. It is* **Philip**.

**Philip** Dominic.

**Philip** *walks past him towards* **Marilyn** *and* **Joseph**, *who stand motionless at the other end of the hall.* **Dominic** *closes the door and puts his back to it, silently watching* **Philip** *and* **Marilyn**.

**Marilyn** I think we'd better just go, Philip.

**Philip** Okay.

**Marilyn** Will you apologise to the others for me, Joseph? I have to go up to my parents' tonight.

**Joseph** (*pathetic*) Of course.

**Marilyn** See you again, I hope. (*She moves to the door,* **Philip** *following.*) I'll be back on Sunday, Dominic. But I'll give you a ring tomorrow night.

**Dominic** *says nothing. He just looks at them, his back to the door.* **Marilyn** *and* **Philip** *move upstairs to get the baby and his things.* **Dominic** *at last leaves the door and goes through to the kitchen/dining room, passing a fantastically uncomfortable* **Joseph** *in the process. He sits down at the table.*

**Joseph** I'm in the way, I know. Can I do anything? I think I should just go and get changed.

**Joseph** *shuffles out awkwardly.* **Dominic** *sits. The sound of the front door closing behind* **Marilyn**, **Philip** *and* **Jack**.

**Siobhan**'s *student house. The middle of the night.*

**Dominic** *and* **Siobhan** *enter the kitchen, having agreed on coffee.* **Siobhan** *is wearing her dressing gown.* **Dominic** *a leather jacket.*

**Siobhan** It's instant.

**Dominic** Thank you.

**Siobhan** Can I ask why you are not at home?

**Dominic** (*the question does not register*) I don't suppose you could manage something to eat, could you?

**Siobhan** Uh –

**Dominic** (*suddenly realising that this is asking a lot*) No, actually, no. Coffee'll be fine.

*There is a long pause.* **Dominic** *stands by the door, as if unwilling to commit himself to staying.* **Siobhan** *is busy with the kettle and the coffee.*

**Siobhan** Does Marilyn know you're here?

**Dominic** No. No, she doesn't.

**Siobhan** I see. (*Not seeing at all.*)

**Dominic** Could I stay? I mean, the spare bed if you like.

*Pause.* **Siobhan** *turns, smiles nervously.*

**Siobhan** There isn't a spare bed.

**Dominic** The floor, then.

**Siobhan** You can sleep in my bed. I'll have the floor. I can sleep anywhere and you look bushed.

**Dominic** Why don't I just borrow your dressing gown and promise to behave? (*Suddenly unsure; he doesn't know what he is doing.*) No, thank you, I must go –

**Siobhan** (*she stops him going*) No, please. It's no problem. Why don't you use the bathroom, and I'll bring the coffee to bed?

**Siobhan** *could do with some reassurance that this is the best plan, but* **Dominic** *shuffles out – obedient rather than keen – to the bathroom.*

**Siobhan**'s *bedroom. A few minutes later.*

**Siobhan** *is sitting up in bed, still wearing the dressing gown. The hall light is on. A shadow arrives, and knocks.*

**Siobhan** Come in.

**Dominic** *comes in. He's wearing only T-shirt and knickers. He carries his clothes in front of himself like a shield.*

**Dominic** I haven't brushed my teeth.

**Siobhan** What?

**Dominic** I can't go to sleep without brushing my teeth.

**Siobhan** Well you can use my toothbrush.

**Dominic** Oh Christ. I'm trying to remember the last time I got into bed with someone else.

**Siobhan** Is Marilyn away? (*No reply.*) Will you not tell me why you've just suddenly turned up?

**Dominic** Dunno.

**Siobhan** Well, can I say I'm happy you did?

**Dominic** Thanks.

*He sits on the edge of the bed. Doesn't know what to do next.* **Siobhan** *hands him the coffee.*

**Siobhan**  Your coffee.

**Dominic**  Oh, right.

**Siobhan**  And you wanted to borrow my dressing gown?

**Dominic**  Yes please.

**Dominic** *sips his coffee and puts the mug down onto the floor. As he is doing this,* **Siobhan** *is removing her dressing gown. When he looks at her again he sees she is naked. He is thrown.*

**Dominic**  Oh.

**Siobhan**  I'm not on the pill, Dominic. That's the only thing.

**Dominic**  Uh. Uh. I have to go now.

**Siobhan**  Why? Because of that? Because I'm not on the pill?

**Dominic**  No. No. Not because of you. No uh – (*Covered in confusion.*) Marilyn's left me, Siobhan.

**Siobhan**  What do you mean, left you? For good?

**Dominic**  Maybe. Well, for the weekend. (*Thinks.*) Maybe. I don't know.

*Long pause. Neither moves.*

**Siobhan** (*struggling for a little dignity*)  Well, there's no reason why you can't sleep here anyway, is there?

**Dominic**  You're really lovely. Do you know that? (*Pause.* **Siobhan** *does not respond. She's hurt.*) Look, I'll call you tomorrow, okay? (*He tries pecking her on the forehead. No response.*) It's just that I'm supposed to have been at a dinner party. And it was *my* dinner party. So I'd better get back and do the washing up. I'll call you tomorr – oh I'm sorry. I'm all over the place tonight. (*Still nothing. He picks up his clothes to leave.*) Sleep tight, eh?

*He leaves.*

*Bristol.* **Philip**'s *new shop. Saturday morning.*

**Philip**, **Marilyn** *and* **Jack** *explore a property in a trendy part of the city. It's part of an old arcade which is being redeveloped and restored. Lovely. Like* **Philip**'s *other shop, this one has living space above.*

**Philip**  Well. What do you think?

**Marilyn**  (*she looks*) It's okay. It'll be nice.

**Philip**  Good, I'm glad. Because I want you to come and live here with me.

**Marilyn** *is shocked. She looks at him.* **Jack** *in her arms, she moves away, through the shop, up to the flat. She surveys the bare rooms.*

**Philip**  (*picking up the conversation again*) I bought this place for us to live in.

**Marilyn**  I don't believe you.

**Philip**  It's true.

**Marilyn**  That's the most absurd thing I've ever heard.

**Philip**  Maybe. (*Calm, logical.*) I wanted to open up another shop. I wanted to live somewhere else. I wanted a life with you. This place came on the market.

**Marilyn**  (*unimpressed*) And now I have? Well, that was useful (*Pause.*) I don't think I'm ready to live with you.

**Philip**  Why not?

**Marilyn**  What about Dominic? What about my job?

**Philip**  (*reasonable*) I want you to come and live here with me. If you want to.

**Marilyn**  He needs changing. (*She means* **Jack** .) I'm sorry. Can we go back to the hotel? He'll sleep. Then we can talk. (*They move to go back.*)

**Philip**  We could sleep.

**Marilyn**  I'm not tired.

**Philip**  We could go to bed anyway.

**Marilyn**  And I'm worried about solving everything in bed.

**Philip**  Why?

**Marilyn**  Because – I don't know. Look Philip . . . Just give me some time. I want to feel . . . (*Doesn't know what she wants to feel.*)

**Philip**  It's okay.

**Marilyn**  Is it? Is it okay? (*She doesn't think it is.*)

**Philip**  I didn't mean –

**Marilyn** (*continuing*)  Because it feels terrible. It feels to me that nothing, that how can anything good come from hurt, from beginning in hurt? and I feel guilty about saying I was going to my parents and then coming here. And not calling . . . I don't know. It doesn't feel okay.

**Philip**  If I thought there was a marriage to break up. If I thought I was destroying something then I wouldn't –

**Marilyn**  Well how could you? If there was a marriage I wouldn't have let you. (*Continuous thought.*) You see, how could Dom see Jack?

**Philip**  It's not that far. It took us two hours to drive here. I want you to know I'll take care of you. And Jack. I promise.

**Marilyn**  Philip, that's not the point.

**Philip** (*simultaneously*)  Wait till you see how well I change nappies.

**Marilyn**  Oh, I can imagine, Philip.

**Philip**  There's nothing here. (*The flat.*) Whatever we did, we could do together. Starting from scratch.

**Marilyn** (*loving him*)  Philip.

**Philip**  What?


*Bristol. Hotel room. Sunday morning.*

**Marilyn**, *in her nightshirt, brings* **Jack** *into the bed. Her side, not* **Philip***'s; he is apparently sleeping.*

**Philip** (*sleepily*)  Hello.

**Marilyn**  I hope you don't mind company.

**Philip**  No.

**Marilyn**  This is a bit of a tradition.

**Philip**  I like it.

**Marilyn**  Do you? Do you mind if he comes in the middle? (*Explaining.*) Then he doesn't fall out.  ˙

**Philip**  No. Of course I don't mind.

**Marilyn** *puts* **Jack** *in the middle.* **Jack** *gurgles and plays with a toy.*

**Marilyn** (*apologetically*) Passion-killer.

**Philip** You think so? (*Wraps his feet round hers.*)

**Marilyn** Do you like him? (**Philip** *smiles.*) Shut up, Marilyn.

**Philip** Yes, I like him. (*Pause.*) And I like you. And I like this dimple, and this mouth. And this nose. (*He touches dimple, mouth, nose.*)

**Marilyn** (*cheerful*) Not these eyes, huh?

**Philip** (*as if making a tough decision*) I quite like the eyes.

**Marilyn** I've got ugly hands. (*Shows them.*)

**Philip** (*holds them*) They're not ugly. They're beautiful.

**Marilyn** No they're not.

**Philip** Okay then, I like your ugly hands.

**Marilyn** (*sternly*) Good. You'd better. Because I can't change them.

**Philip** And I like here. (*Touching under the quilt.*) And here. (*He puts his hand to her breast.*)

**Marilyn** (*laughing*) Get off!

**Philip** I mention no names in front of the infant.

**Marilyn** I'm glad.

**Philip** Hm?

**Marilyn** Thanks for this time. It's been good.

**Philip** It has. It has been good. Can I hold one of your ugly hands? (*They hold hands.*) The thing is, Marilyn, you can stay with Dominic, and feel righteous, and nobody will blame you, and you'll maybe survive. Or you can come to me, and everybody will blame you, and it will involve all kinds of pain, but if you do come, it will be because you want to come, and it will be honest. And Dominic will gain – I think – because he will be forced to consider what he really wants, and not just drift along, which he does. He plays at being married, and that's not good enough for you.

**Marilyn** But he loves me, Philip. And he thinks it's good enough for him.

**Philip** How does he know?

**Marilyn** How do you?

**Philip** I can feel you. I can feel how much of your heart is going spare.

**Marilyn** (*loving him*) Can you?

**Philip** Yes.

*They kiss.* **Jack** *gurgles.*


*Outside* **Dominic/Marilyn**'*s house. Monday morning.*

*From his study window,* **Dominic** *watches* **Marilyn**, **Philip** *and* **Jack** *arrive in* **Philip**'*s car.* **Marilyn** *and* **Philip** *unload.*

**Philip** Good luck. Do you want me to come in with you?

**Marilyn** No. I'll call you.

**Marilyn** *turns with no gesture of affection, and enters the house.* **Philip** *looks up suddenly at* **Dominic**'*s study window. An impulsive wave as he meets* **Dominic**'*s stare.* **Dominic** *reciprocates, equally impulsive – then catches himself in mid-wave. A beat.* **Philip** *gets into the car and drives off.*

**Marilyn** *goes into the kitchen/dining area.* **Dominic** *has cleaned up: everything is spotless, immaculate. A vase of flowers on the table. She puts* **Jack** *in his chair and sets about making him some food.* **Dominic** *comes in and goes straight to* **Jack**.

**Dominic** Hello, fish face! How have you been? (*Pretends to listen to* **Jack**'*s reply.*) Did you? Oh, have you? Well, I didn't have such a good time. I went down the swings. Played hide-and-seek, blind man's buff: usual sort of weekend. (*Excited.*) Oh! I did some drawing and colouring in!

**Marilyn** Dominic. (*He has ignored her so far.*)

**Dominic** (*lightly*) Hi. Good weekend?

**Marilyn** I don't think good or bad comes into it.

**Dominic** Really? How odd. What does come into it?

**Marilyn** (*ignoring this*) Were you all right? Did you manage? I intended to come back last night, but . . .

**Dominic** (*not listening; notices that* **Jack** *is wearing new dungarees*) Are these new?

**Marilyn** Yes. They're lovely, aren't they?

**Dominic** (*to* **Jack**) Oh, they're pretty sexy. (*Looking at him, admiring.*) Do you think he looks like me today?

**Marilyn** Everybody says so. Will you have some coffee?

**Dominic** How are your folks?

**Marilyn** I didn't see them.

**Dominic** Oh?

**Marilyn** You knew that.

**Dominic** (*in mock confusion*) No, sorry. I thought you'd said you were going down to your parents for a few days. To think.

**Marilyn** Dominic. I spoke to my mother last night. She told me you'd spoken to her.

**Dominic** Right.

**Marilyn** So why did you ask me how she was?

**Dominic** (*ignoring the question*) Oh, incidentally, one thing that can be said for heartbreak: it's great copy.

**Marilyn** Please, Dom.

**Dominic** No really, it's true. (*He is speaking as if he is still telling* **Jack** *about his weekend.*) Last night, of course, I expected you back. So while I kept vigil; the drawings! Well, I couldn't stop. And some of them are very funny, though I say so myself. (**Jack** *cries.*) Oh all right, then: quite funny.

**Marilyn** I have to go to work.

**Dominic** Right, back to the gallery.

**Marilyn** No.

**Dominic** I must say, on reflection, I was pretty dim, wasn't I? When Philip suggested hanging that exhibition in his gallery, I thought, that was terribly philanthropic. I thought (*Enjoying this alliteration.*) how philanthropic of Philip. There you go.

**Marilyn** (*persevering*) Thanks for making everything so tidy. It's beautiful. And the flowers.

**Dominic** Right.

**Marilyn** Why did you have to wait until now to do it?

**Dominic** (**Marilyn** *had made* **Jack**'s *food*) Can I feed him?

**Marilyn** Of course.

**Dominic** (*to* **Jack**, *cooing*) 'Cause I missed him. I missed you, brat face. There was nothing to do all night except sleep.

**Marilyn** Listen, I won't go to work this morning. I'll ring the office. We could take him out for a walk. How does that sound?

**Dominic** Okay.

**Marilyn** Okay. I'll go and call. I really think we need to talk. (**Dominic** *does not look at her. Continues feeding* **Jack** .) Dom? (*No response. She gives up.*) I'll go and call.

*Approach to a children's playground. The same morning.*

**Dominic** *and* **Marilyn** *are pushing* **Jack** *towards the playground. It is cold. They are less tense.*

**Dominic** So where did you go? Or do you not want to discuss that? I don't mind.

**Marilyn** It's okay. Bristol.

**Dominic** What, a hotel?

**Marilyn** Yes.

**Dominic** Mr and Mrs Philip?

**Marilyn** Shut up.

**Dominic** Did you have to take Jack with you?

**Marilyn** Come on Dominic. He's never spent a night apart from me. Apart from anything else it's pretty obvious we have a dependency on each other. I've hardly stopped feeding him.

**Dominic** What's the difference between your being responsible to Jack and being responsible to me?

*They reach the park. They nod at a mum they both know.*

**Marilyn** Look, are we really going to talk? In which case, let's go home and talk.

**Dominic** (*loud, embarrassing*) I don't want you to leave me. Can I make that clear? Am I making that clear? I don't want you to leave me.

**Marilyn** Dominic.

**Dominic** And I don't want you in somebody else's bed. And I particularly don't want my son in someone else's bed. (*Pause. Thinks.*) Oh God, I've just thought of that. Did he go in the bed with you? Christ.

**Marilyn** No.

**Dominic** Christ.

**Marilyn** *is holding* **Jack** *in her arms. She sits on the roundabout. Pushes it a little.*

**Marilyn** Philip is going to move to Bristol. He wants us to move with him.

**Dominic** Does he.

**Marilyn** You're telling me what you want. I'm telling you what he wants.

**Dominic** Why should what he wants figure in our marriage? In our family?

**Marilyn** Let's go back, Dom. It's not fair to do this out here.

**Dominic** Fair? Is it fair you're not giving us a chance?

**Marilyn** I've given us *years*.

**Dominic** (*desperate*) I love you. I need you.

**Marilyn** (*suddenly*) Do you want me to say I won't see Philip?

**Dominic** What?

**Marilyn** I could try not seeing him.

**Dominic** What's the point? What's the point if you don't want to?

**Marilyn** I don't know. Let's go back, eh?

**Dominic** (*sullen*) No, I think I'll stay here. I'll see you later.

**Marilyn** Oh Dominic. Okay.

**Dominic** Will you leave the baby? (*She opens her mouth to express doubts, but he anticipates.*) I haven't been with him. I want to be. Just for a few minutes. I'll bring him back.

**Marilyn** They said it was going to rain, Dom. I don't want him to get wet.

**Dominic** (*slowly*) Yes, well, if it rains we'll come back straight away.

*She gives* **Dominic** *the baby. He holds him tight. Sits on the roundabout.* **Marilyn** *hesitates, then turns and walks away.* **Dominic** *and* **Jack** *spin slowly on the roundabout.*

# Part Two

*Outside* **Dominic/Marilyn**'*s house. Early evening. Some weeks later.*

**Dominic** *drives up in the Beetle and gets out.* **Marilyn** *greets him at the car. She's holding the baby. She has her coat on, ready to go out:* **Dominic** *has agreed to baby-sit for her.*

**Marilyn** (*warmly*) Hello.

**Dominic** (*business-like*) What time will you be back? (*Hands* **Marilyn** *the car keys.*) It needs petrol.

**Marilyn** (*concerned*) Are you okay, Dom?

**Dominic** (*business-like*) Tremendous. (*He takes* **Jack** *from her.*) We'll see you later.

**Dominic** *carries* **Jack** *into the house.* **Marilyn** *sighs and gets into the car.*

**Philip**'*s flat. Early evening.*

**Marilyn** *and* **Philip** *are in the process of packing up* **Philip**'*s belongings for the move to Bristol. His things are being divided up into those which will be sold in the new shop, and those which will be kept as ornaments or whatever.*

**Philip** *is considering a beautiful African figure. It is an old man carved in wood, three feet tall, smiling benignly.*

**Marilyn** (*horrified*) You can't sell him!

**Philip** I think we'll need the space.

**Marilyn** Why?

**Philip** Your stuff. The baby's. It's not that big a space.

**Marilyn** There won't be that much. I don't want to take any of the things from the house.

**Philip** I see. (*He hadn't realised this.*)

**Marilyn** Well, obviously things that are mine, were mine before. But nothing else.

**Philip** Okay.

**Marilyn** Because he's losing me and Jack. It's not fair he should lose anything else.

**Philip** Hey, why are you telling me all this? Marilyn, it's you I want, not your fridge-freezer.

*They hug.*

**Marilyn** Sometimes I wish I could rub everything out and start again with us.

**Philip** And the baby.

**Marilyn** And the baby.

**Philip** Dominic?

*She disengages.*

**Marilyn** I don't know. Maybe I don't wish that.

**Philip** Is work all right? Are they going to give you a watch? (*As a leaving present.*)

**Marilyn** Probably. (*Pause.*) Gossip is rampant. For a charitable organisation, it doesn't manage much between its staff.

**Philip** And Dominic? Has he agreed to meet us somewhere?

**Marilyn** I haven't asked him. I'm sorry. I will. It's just – if I dwell on him I can't move . . . He paralyses me. He's paralysed. I'll get back tonight and he'll go as soon as I walk through the door. He won't talk. Have you read this month's *Harpers*?

**Philip** Why? No, should I?

**Marilyn** There's a cartoon.

**Philip** And?

**Marilyn** Well, of course, the thing is, if you didn't know about us it wouldn't mean anything. But it's pretty hurtful.

**Philip** Well, it's understandable.

**Marilyn** Yes. Just stings a bit, that's all.

**Philip** That's all (*Wry smile.*)

**Marilyn** That's all. (*Wry smile.*)

**Dominic/Marilyn**'s *house. The same time*

**Dominic** *has an ironing board out.* **Siobhan** *sits at the table, watching him iron his clothes. He's baby-sitting while* **Marilyn** *sees* **Philip**. *She's baby-sitting him. And he needs it. Despite* **Siobhan**'s *efforts,* **Dominic**

*remains steadfastly grim-faced.*

**Siobhan**  I don't understand you ironing clothes and then shoving them into a holdall.

**Dominic**  I like ironing.

**Siobhan**  Well, why not iron some of Marilyn's things and do yours when you get back to Chris's?

**Dominic**  If I iron Marilyn's clothes, she'll think I'm getting at her. She hates ironing.

**Siobhan**  So do I. It's a historical thing.

**Dominic**  What is?

**Siobhan**  Women hating ironing. Centuries of oppression.

**Dominic**  There haven't been irons for centuries.

**Siobhan**  Oh yes there have.

**Dominic**  Yeah. I suppose so. Look, I just like ironing. I find it therapeutic. Okay?

**Siobhan**  I think you hide behind it. It's like a weapon. Don't come close or you'll get your fingers burned.

**Dominic**  Maybe.

**Siobhan**  You want me to go, don't you? Before Marilyn comes back.

**Dominic**  (*not entirely honest*)  No.

**Siobhan**  Doesn't fit the victim bill to have me around.

**Dominic**  Hey. Don't. And I don't want to be a victim.

**Siobhan**  Then why did you move out?

**Dominic**  Uh –

**Siobhan**  And why have you done nothing, gone nowhere, for weeks? Told no one what's happened? (*Gently.*) Why won't you sleep with me?

**Dominic**  I dunno.

**Siobhan**  You won't sleep with me because it means you'd have nothing over Marilyn. You couldn't feel self-righteous.

**Dominic**  No. I'm sorry you feel like that. I don't feel that's what I'm doing.

**Siobhan**  It is what you're doing, Dom. You string me along. I mean, why come and sleep in my bed – because you do *sleep* with me – so why not *touch* me? It makes me feel repellent to you.

**Dominic** (*weakly*) You're not. You're beautiful. (*He continues to iron.*)

**Siobhan** Iron, iron.

**Dominic** (*looks at her. Irons. Shrugs*) Iron, iron.

**Siobhan** And it's ridiculous baby-sitting while Marilyn sees Philip. (*Long pause.* **Dominic** *ironing.*) I'm going to the Lake District next week. Why don't you come?

**Dominic** No thanks. I've got work to do.

**Siobhan** Yes. I saw (*Bitterly.*) Am I the ageing virgin? (*Referring to the illustration in Harpers.*)

**Dominic** Ah! Is that why you're being like this?

**Siobhan** Why are you doing that rubbish?

**Dominic** Fame and fortune. I get propositioned in the supermarket.

**Siobhan** Yes, it *is* why I'm being like this. For the record. I just don't understand why you won't talk, but you do this oblique slagging off of Philip and Marilyn in print. It, it stinks.

**Dominic** Yeah.

**Siobhan** (*sharply*) And putting yourself down in the process doesn't mitigate that!

**Dominic** No.

**Siobhan** No!

**Dominic** What time is it?

**Siobhan** (*demolished*) It's all right. I'm going. (*She gets up very quickly and almost runs to the door.*)

**Dominic** (*not wanting her to go*) No. I just –

**Siobhan** (*coming back in, thawing*) I'm sorry. I didn't intend to lose my temper. I'm sorry. I know it's . . . well, you know I know. And you can come round if you can't sleep and put your head on my shoulder. And toss and turn all night, and peck me on the cheek and that's fine and I won't tell anyone. (*Pause.*) And iron bloody iron.

*She goes.* **Dominic** *shrugs. Irons.*

**Dominic**'s *room. Later that evening.*

**Dominic** *is drawing.* **Marilyn** *appears, cautious.*

**Marilyn** Hi.

**Dominic** Hi.

*He immediately starts collecting his pens and equipment. Gathers his drawings together, puts them into an art folder.*

**Marilyn** Did he get off all right?

**Dominic** Yep.

**Marilyn** And he ate everything?

**Dominic** Yeah. He was great.

**Marilyn** Good. Thanks for –

**Dominic** (*cutting her off*) Right. Okay. I could come over tomorrow if you want to go out.

**Marilyn** Yes. Thanks. (*Struggling.*) I mean, I don't know if I will but you can come over anyway . . . I mean obviously, you know, whatever.

**Dominic** I did some ironing.

**Marilyn** I saw. Thanks.

**Dominic** I was doing some of my own, so –

**Marilyn** I said thank you.

**Dominic** No. No, I just meant . . . Forget it. I'll see you.

**Marilyn** Am I supposed to feel guilty because you ironed some of my clothes? Because I washed all of your clothes for *years.*

**Dominic** (*doesn't want to hear*) Okay.

**Marilyn** I just didn't tell you every day. 'I washed some of your clothes today'. Didn't seem very interesting.

**Dominic** Yeah, well I go to the launderette now. It's terrific. I get a service wash. I get clean clothes without the poison in the final rinse. (*He has all his things. Puts on his jacket.*)

**Marilyn** Well, that's all right then.

**Dominic** Absolutely. So, if you'd ring me at Chris's and let me know whether you'll be out or not tomorrow.

*He goes past her to leave.* **Marilyn** *grabs him, tugging on his jacket.*

**Marilyn** Is this it? Dominic? Is this how we're going to be with each other?

**Dominic** (*the victim*) I don't know.

**Marilyn** (*exasperated*) Christ, Dominic! Why won't you talk, say something?

**Dominic** Like?

**Marilyn** Like, what's going on? I do actually care about you, you know. About where you are. How you're coping. If you're sleeping. Your parents . . .

**Dominic** (*exaggerated sarcasm*) Oh, we're *fine*. How are you? And your parents?

**Marilyn** Oh, Christ!

**Dominic** Marilyn, listen. You've ditched me for someone else. It's perfectly clear, isn't it? What's there to discuss? Whether I like it? I don't. Whether I'm happy? I'm not. That's about it, isn't it?

**Marilyn** (*quietly*) Yes. But for me to know that, you needed to tell me.

**Dominic** Oh, right. I've got it. Sorry. Right. Well let's just write this up on the wall, shall we?

*He removes a picture from the wall by the door. Takes a thick, indelible felt marker. Scribbles 'DON'T GO!' on the wall.*

Okay? Is that clear? Can you read that?

**Marilyn** (*close to tears*) I can read it. But I don't believe the things you write. To tell you the truth.

**Dominic** What?

**Marilyn** I think your cartoon strip in that magazine is cheap. And it hurts me.

**Dominic** (*not entirely honest*) It's not about you.

**Marilyn** (*disbelieving*) No.

**Dominic** No.

**Marilyn** No, the desperate virgin.

**Dominic** Oh God. Right Marilyn, can I just say one thing here before I piss off again to make way for your lover – whom I assume comes complete with washing machine – and that is, if there's one thing about you which hurts me, it is your infinite capacity to absorb any pain, or admission, or any, or, I mean it just doesn't seem to make any odds: you just *soak* it up. (*Looking her in the face. Quite cruel.*) My sense of you, is of this moving sponge which travels purposefully in a single direction, and will just sort of sponge right over me. Irrespective of what I say or do.

**Marilyn** (*stung, fighting back the tears*) I don't feel like a sponge. I care about you. I worry about you. But I don't think I want to live with you. Is staying with you the only way I can show you I care?

**Dominic** You want to go, you go. I won't give you permission to leave. I won't drag our marriage around like some cripple. If you don't want me – us – you jigger off.

*He picks up his things for a second time, and leaves.* **Marilyn** *sinks into the couch.*

**Chris**'s *flat. Later that evening.*

**Dominic** *is slumped in the front room of* **Chris**'s *flat.* **Chris** *has been putting* **Dominic** *up for the past few weeks.* **Chris** *is a long-standing loyal friend. He affects a boorish, abrasive, chauvinist manner. While* **Dominic** *slumps,* **Chris** *scoffs a takeaway Chicken Tikka Masala at the coffee table. He's just come back from his evening class in typing.*

**Chris** You sure you don't want some of this? It's good.

**Dominic** Positive.

**Chris** You got to eat, Dom.

**Dominic** I have.

**Chris** So've I. But I'm so depressed about that typing class, I had to eat again.

**Dominic** Why do you do it if you hate it so much?

**Chris** I hate the class. I'm in love with the women.

**Dominic** Which women?

**Chris** All of them. All of them. There are a dozen nubiles with magnificent chubbies. All different species and under twenty. That's why I'm so depressed. (*Considers the food.*) I can't eat all of this. D'you know one of them's called Gloria. Can you imagine it? There are actually girls called Gloria. She smiled at me like I was her uncle. Then I thought – well, I *could* be her uncle. She showed me how to set my margins.

**Dominic** And why typing anyway?

**Chris** Typing's a brain-wave. Only young girls, gay men and me want to do it. Anyway, I'm giving it up. I can't do it, and (*Sitting back, full.*) I'm getting fat. (*Pause, nervous.*) How was *your* night?

**Dominic** Hopeless.

**Chris** Right. Look, Dom. When Janet left me, that was it. End. Finish. Full stop. But with you, half the neighbourhood is queuing up as a substitute.

**Dominic** That's not true.

**Chris** What about the student: Siobhan?

**Dominic** One person is not a queue.

**Chris** And what's-her-name was round here like a flash with the Red Cross parcel, crooning all over you.

**Dominic** She wasn't. She was just being kind.

**Chris** (*doubtful*) Yeah.

**Dominic** Anyway, that's only two.

**Chris** Christ, it's early days yet. All I got was spaghetti bolognese round at your house and Marilyn being smug.

**Dominic** She wasn't smug.

**Chris** She *was* smug. So were you as a matter of fact. You sort of crouched in a concerned way. It really pissed me off.

**Dominic** Thanks a lot.

**Chris** Well. I wanted alcohol and help slagging Janet off.

**Dominic** She's a great woman, and you know it.

**Chris** Christ! See what I mean? And she's okay. She's not great.

**Dominic** I'm not going to criticise Marilyn. What's the point?

**Chris** Or Philip? You'd think he was a saint, listening to you. (*Pause.*) They're trampling all over you, Dominic, and you know it.

**Dominic** No.

**Chris** Well yes, actually. Look, you're baby-sitting while your wife goes out screwing and you don't think you're being trampled on. You move out so that she doesn't get inconvenienced. Come on, Dom. It's a farce.

**Dominic**  Am I in the way or something?

**Chris**  Get drunk! Hit somebody! Philip preferably. Or Marilyn. But talk about it. Have a breakdown or something. But let it out for Christ-sakes. It's like living with a shaken up coke can.

**Dominic** (*shouting*)  Is it!

**Chris** (*shouting*)  Yes it is!

**Dominic** (*thawing, almost laughing, shouting*)  Well, I'm sorry.

**Chris** (*shouting, laughing*)  And I'm sorry. (*Quieter.*) It's a bugger what's happening to you and Jack.

**Dominic** (*subdued again at the mention of* **Jack**)  Yeah. Anyway. I'm going out.

**Chris**  Siobhan's place?

**Dominic**  Dunno. Maybe. (*He dips a chapati into the curry.*)

**Chris**  Finish it.

**Dominic**  No. (*But he dips in another piece.*)

**Chris**  Finish it! Look, Dom. Go round to that beautiful woman, get laid, and be grateful.

*Outside* **Dominic/Marilyn**'s *house. Later that night.*

**Philip**'s *car is parked outside the house.* **Dominic** *is standing across the street, watching. There's nothing much to watch. He's been there a long time. A neighbour walks by with a dog. A light comes on in the house, upstairs. Silhouette of* **Philip***. Then* **Marilyn***. A kiss. Then the light goes off again.* **Dominic** *walks across the streets to* **Philip**'s *car. He kicks the door panel as hard as he can. He is immediately embarrassed. Bends down to examine the dent. He rubs at it. Looks about him furtively. Then slinks off down the road.*

*Health Food Shop Cafeteria. A Saturday afternoon some days later.*

**Philip** *and* **Marilyn** *have been doing some shopping for the new flat. Bags and treats around the table of salads and other worthy food.* **Jack** *is in a high-chair, next to* **Philip***, who is feeding him.* **Marilyn** *is restless, distracted:* **Dominic** *is outside.*

**Marilyn** Philip, he's still there, across the street. I'm going to go out and say something to him.

**Philip** I don't think you'll have to. (**Dominic** *is making his way towards the cafe.*)

**Marilyn** Oh, Christ. I sometimes think he gets some kind of kick – (*Trails off and looks down.*)

**Philip** Marilyn. (*No response.*) Marilyn. (*He squeezes her hand. She looks at him.*) It's us. We're okay. It's okay.

**Dominic** *arrives at the table.*

**Dominic** The market's very good here. What did you buy, anything nice?

**Philip** Will you join us?

**Dominic** Why not? (*He sits down.*) I'll sit next to my son.

**Marilyn** Do you want some food?

**Dominic** Oh, I don't think so. Looks a bit too pious for me. (*Looks at their bags.*) A lampshade!

**Philip** We're shopping for the flat in Bristol.

**Dominic** Yes, I'd guessed.

*Pause.*

**Marilyn** Dominic, if you don't want to eat, what do you want? –

**Dominic** I stood outside for half an hour. I thought you might have found the time to come out and talk to me.

**Marilyn** I didn't see you.

**Philip** I did, Dominic. I just didn't know what you were hoping for.

**Dominic** Good old Philip, eh? Honest to a fault. (*Mock query.*) Is that the expression?

**Philip** I think there's a facetious response to anything I might say to you, Dominic.

**Dominic** (*fast, bitter*) You're right. Yes, there is. (*To* **Marilyn**.) So. *We* came to this market to get the things for the baby, remember?

**Marilyn** Yes.

**Dominic** And then here. You couldn't eat properly because your bulge kept bashing the table.

**Philip** (*intervening*) Would you prefer it if we left? We could find somewhere to talk. You could come back to the gallery.

**Marilyn** It wasn't this cafe. Not that it matters. But for the record. It wasn't this cafe.

**Dominic** It doesn't really matter which cafe it was, does it?

**Marilyn** (*speechless*) Well . . .

**Dominic** No. (*To* **Philip**.) I came to see you. They told me at your gallery I'd find you here.

**Philip** Right.

**Dominic** I owe you some money for the damage to your car. Can I write you a cheque? (*Reaches inside his jacket for the cheque book.*)

**Philip** It took me five minutes to get the dent out. It didn't cost anything.

**Dominic** (*replacing the cheque book*) Of course. I forgot you'd be able to do things like that. Anyway, I'm not proud of what happened.

**Philip** I don't blame you. Forget it.

**Dominic** (*aggressive*) I mean, if I'd kicked *you*, at least it would seem less like just – petulance, don't you think?

**Philip** Yeah.

**Marilyn** Let's go, shall we?

**Dominic** (*exaggerated politeness*) No, listen, don't let me stop you doing whatever it was you were doing. Really, I mean let's be civilised.

**Philip** You're not stopping us doing what we're doing. But why don't we try and talk about what's happened?

**Dominic** You see, there's another thing which you're good at which I just can't do.

**Philip** What's that?

**Dominic** Making life into conversation. Marilyn can do it, of course. The *two* of you must have a great time – all that sponge stuff –

**Marilyn** For God's sake, Dominic!

**Dominic** Exchanging liquids. Dribbling into each other.

**Philip** Dominic!

**Marilyn** Don't get involved, Philip.

**Philip** It's all right. I don't feel that's what I'm doing. (*To* **Dominic**.) I don't know of any other way of communicating with you without using words. I know you're hurt. I know this hurts you. And I'm sorry. But we're in love, and we want to be together, and Marilyn's going to come and live with me in Bristol. And that directly involves you, and I want you to know about it, and if it means that we have to talk in a restaurant on a Saturday afternoon, then so be it. I don't think that ignoring the reality and playing, or whatever it is that's happening. –

*As* **Philip** *trails off, a woman,* **Jenny,** *comes up behind* **Dominic** *and puts her hands round his eyes. Her husband,* **Malcolm,** *stands droopily behind her with* **Josephine,** *their sixteen-year-old daughter.*

**Jenny** Guess who? (*Beams at* **Marilyn**.) Don't say. (**Marilyn** *doesn't say. Neither does* **Philip**. **Dominic** *has begun weeping into* **Jenny**'s *hands*.) Do you want a clue? (*She teases*.) Somebody who's very angry with you, because you promised to come and see us and show us your baby. And then you didn't come to see me in my Gilbert and Sullivan either. Is it because you're too famous now? (*She giggles. No response from* **Dominic**. **Philip** *and* **Marilyn** *are paralysed*.) And Malcolm, Malcolm saw your cartoons in *Harpers* and thought they were very wicked! Guessed? No? (*Laughing to* **Philip**.) Don't worry, I'm not from the loony bin. (*To* **Dominic**.) Come on! Guess! I'm not going to take my hands away until you've guessed who this is!

**Malcolm** (*uncomfortable*) He knows. I think. (*To* **Marilyn**.) Hello.

**Jenny** No, he's got to guess! (**Dominic** *shudders uncontrollably*.) Are you laughing?

**Marilyn** Jenny, I really don't think this . . .

**Jenny** Oh Marilyn! You've spoiled it. You –

**Philip** I'm sorry but Dominic's not been feeling well. Perhaps he could call you later.

**Jenny** What?

**Dominic** *covers his eyes with his own hands, keeps his head down.*

**Malcolm** I'm sorry . . . Jenny's . . .

**Philip** Please. Do you think you might –?

**Malcolm**  Let's go, Jenny. I'm sorry Marilyn. We'll give you a bell.

**Jenny** (*cooing she's spotted the baby*)  Is that the baby? A little boy! (*To* **Marilyn**.) What do you call him?

**Marilyn**  Jack.

**Jenny**  Lovely. Well bye little Jack . . . Marilyn. (*To* **Philip**.) Nice to have met you. (*She pats* **Dominic**'s *head*.) Well, we're off. (*To* **Marilyn**.) We're buying Josephine a dress.

**Marilyn**  Great.

**Jenny**  She's going to a disco tonight. Wearing my shoes! Can you imagine! It's lovely to see you again. Bye-bye Jack. Very handsome!

*The retreat is completed.* **Marilyn** *and* **Philip** *sit in silence.* **Dominic** *sits, head slumped, sobbing into his hands.*

**Philip** (*to* **Marilyn**)  Are you going to eat any of this?

**Marilyn**  I'm not hungry.

**Philip**  Shall we have a coffee? Dominic, would you like a cup of coffee? (**Dominic** *nods in his hands.*)

**Philip** *gets up.* **Marilyn** *puts a comforting arm around* **Dominic**. *He keeps his head down.*

**Dominic/Marilyn**'s *house. The next evening.*

**Marilyn** *is on her knees in the sitting room, sorting out books and records into two piles, hers and* **Dominic**'s. **Dominic** *returns, having put* **Jack** *to bed.*

**Dominic**  He was really exhausted. He almost dropped off when I was drying him after the bath. (*He kneels down by the books.*) Which pile's yours?

**Marilyn**  This one.

**Dominic** *takes a book from 'his' pile.*

**Dominic**  Oh. Is this mine?

**Marilyn**  Well . . . it was a Christmas present to us both from your aunt in Greenwich. I think that means you keep it.

**Dominic**  I've never looked at it. Do you want it?

**Marilyn**  No.

**Dominic**  (*as they continue sorting*)  What's happening about the move?

**Marilyn**  Philip's coming with a van in the morning.

**Dominic**  Tomorrow?

*Pause.*

**Marilyn**  Yeah.

**Dominic**  A van full, huh?

**Marilyn**  There's all Jack's things. His cot, and stuff. And the highchair.

**Dominic**  Right.

*They continue.*

**Marilyn**  You don't have to do this, Dom. I can manage.

**Dominic**  It's okay. What else are you taking besides your books?

**Marilyn**  Oh, maybe my records. Some clothes.

**Dominic**  What about furniture?

**Marilyn**  Well, I don't know. What do you think?

**Dominic**  (*meaning it*)  Take whatever you want.

**Marilyn**  Actually, the thing which I'd . . . I could really do with, but I mean, obviously if . . .

**Dominic**  What?

**Marilyn**  The bed.

**Dominic**  (*this registers*)  Right.

**Marilyn**  It's just that I mean you know it's what I need for my back and the one Philip has is no good and . . .

**Dominic**  No, take it. (*Pause.*)  I probably wouldn't be able to sleep in it again anyway.

**Marilyn**  It's a bed, Dominic.

**Dominic**  Yeah.

**Marilyn**  But thanks. That's kind.

**Dominic**  Listen, Marilyn. I don't care. It's not kindness. You're going. Jack's going. The possessions – the things in this place –

are neither here nor there. If I come back tomorrow and the house is empty, it really wouldn't bother me.

**Marilyn** Well obviously, there's no question –

**Dominic** Oh, I'd like to keep the stereo.

**Marilyn** (*she wanted it*) Okay.

**Dominic** Unless you particularly . . .

**Marilyn** No its fine. Could I have the radio-cassette then?

**Dominic** Fine.

**Marilyn** And I would be grateful if I could have the washing machine.

**Dominic** (*surprised*) Philip doesn't have one?

**Marilyn** No. And there's all the baby's stuff . . . nappies and, well, you know, there's half a house to wash every day. I really couldn't manage without –

**Dominic** No, no. I said . . . whatever you want.

**Marilyn** I'd rather you knew what I was taking. And agree.

**Dominic** What about the car?

**Marilyn** I don't know.

**Marilyn** *wants the car. So does* **Dominic**. *He's also begun to contemplate all the other things he'd like to keep.*

**Dominic** Well, the thing is, if you take the car, how do I get to see Jack? (*A pause.*) That is allowed?

**Marilyn** Don't be stupid. You know you can see him as much as you like.

**Dominic** Every day? (*No response.*) Anyway, that's the problem as regards the car.

*Pause.*

**Marilyn** It's very easy by train.

**Dominic** Yeah, but when I get the other end, then what?

**Marilyn** In what sense?

**Dominic** Well, do I have to say yes or no this minute?

**Marilyn** Well obviously not.

*There's a sheet of paper on the floor.* **Dominic** *picks it up, examines it.*

**Dominic**  Is this the list of things you wanted to take with you?

**Marilyn**  I mean, I hadn't actually intended for you to read it. It's just to jog my thoughts.

**Dominic**  (*looking down the list*)  Doesn't Philip have cutlery?

**Marilyn**  I don't know. I don't want to be dependent on him. I'd rather have things which . . . Anyway, we got two sets from our wedding presents. You don't need them both.

**Dominic**  No. I guess not. It's just that there are things here which I won't have but I'm sure Philip already has. The liquidiser . . . uh – the radio alarm – surely you don't want that? So you end up with two of something and ...

**Marilyn**  He doesn't actually have a liquidiser, but anyway.

**Dominic**  (*putting down the list*)  Look, this is silly. If I read this list I'll get . . . I'm getting frazzled here. I mean it when I say I'd prefer you just took the stuff . . . I probably won't even notice it's gone. Actually, I'll tell you what you *can* take.

**Marilyn**  What's that?

**Dominic**  The lawn mower.

**Marilyn**  Why?

**Dominic**  Haven't you got a garden in Bristol?

**Marilyn**  Hardly.

**Dominic**  Well, it'll come in handy.

**Marilyn**  What about the lawn? I bought you that lawn mower.

**Dominic**  I'll pay a boy-scout to cut it once a year.

**Marilyn**  He'll still have to have something to cut it with.

**Dominic**  I don't care. He can use his teeth.

*Pause.*

**Marilyn**  Why didn't you say?

**Dominic**  That I hate gardening?

**Marilyn**  Yes.

**Dominic**  (*slowly*)  Or decorating? Or rambles? Or holidays? Or exhibitions?

**Marilyn** Yes, if you do!

**Dominic** Because there's not much else, is there, of the things you enjoy?

**Marilyn** How did we get to here, Dominic?

**Dominic** I think that at one point we were in love. Wasn't that it?

**Marilyn** I need a drink. How about you?

**Dominic** I'll get it. What?

**Marilyn** Anything.

**Dominic** Can I say something to you, Marilyn. Since you – over the last few weeks – or perhaps I've just started looking at you . . . anyway, you look lovely. You look great. (*A pause.*) I know what we'll drink.

*He springs up, goes to the cupboard and hunts. He finds an ancient bottle of champagne. Takes it, and two glasses.*

**Marilyn** (*smiling*) You can't resist it, can you?

**Dominic** What?

**Marilyn** Yes, okay, let's drink that.

**Dominic** Listen, I can't see us celebrating our silver wedding anniversary together. So let's celebrate this, eh?

**Marilyn** I don't mind.

**Dominic** Right. (*He opens the bottle. There is no pop.*) Oh it's flat. How appropriate. (*Pours anyway.*) To . . . something.

**Marilyn** To something. (*They drink.*) Will you get a lodger to move in here?

**Dominic** No idea?

**Marilyn** Or sell it?

**Dominic** You worried about the money?

**Marilyn** Not at the moment, no.

**Dominic** Then I've no idea what I'm going to do. And I don't want to think about it. And the Joan Armatrading's mine, I think.

**Marilyn** It's mine.

**Dominic** Then there must be two copies, because I know I had one.

**Marilyn** (*incredulous*) You didn't!

**Dominic** Yes. I did.

**Marilyn** One of the reasons you moved in with me was because I had that record!

**Dominic** It was the Vivaldi I coveted.

**Marilyn** And the Joan Armatrading! Christ!

**Dominic** Well, you never listen to them; you take the covers, and I'll keep the records.

**Marilyn** (*raging now*) Dominic, you sort out which records you want. As you're keeping the stereo it makes no odds.

**Dominic** (*placating*) Hey.

**Marilyn** You seem to find this easy. I don't. And I don't want to have an inquest over each thing in the house. Or be reminded that it has a history.

**Dominic** Why not?

**Marilyn** When did we last talk this much?

*Pause.*

**Dominic** I don't know.

**Marilyn** And why has it taken this?

*She goes into the kitchen.* **Dominic** *goes to the stereo and plays the Joan Armatrading record. The song is 'Love and Affection'. He turns the volume up loud. Pours himself another glass of flat champagne.*

**Dominic/Marilyn** *'s house: the bathroom. Later that evening.*

**Marilyn** *is soaking in the bath.* **Dominic** *comes in without warning. She covers herself.*

**Dominic** Yes. Isn't that funny? We can't be naked. I'm sorry, I just wanted to wash your back.

**Marilyn** (*she moves down the bath, presenting him with her back*) Thanks. Go ahead.

**Dominic** *takes a sponge and sits on the edge of the tub. He begins to wash her back, slowly, lovingly.*

**Dominic**  You didn't lock the door.

**Marilyn**  I didn't expect you to come in. You never would, even when I asked.

**Dominic**  Well, no.

*Pause.*

**Marilyn**  I'm sorry. (*She means for everything.*)

**Dominic**  (*very gently*)  So am I, Marilyn. (*He kisses the centre of her back.*)

**Marilyn**  (*embarrassed*)  Hey.

**Dominic**  I do love you, Marilyn. (*He kisses her again, leaning more and more into the bath, getting wet. He is fully clothed.*)

**Marilyn**  Don't.

**Dominic**  Marilyn, please. (*He embraces her from behind.*)

**Marilyn**  (*resisting*)  Oh look, don't please. (*She clambers out, grabs a towel. As she does so,* **Dominic** *half slips, half flops into the bath.*)  I'm sorry. I can't. I'm sorry.

*She exits, embarrassed, upset.* **Dominic** *stretches out in the bath.*


**Dominic/Marilyn**'s *house. The following day.*

**Dominic** *arrives at the house, lets himself in.* **Marilyn** *has left. The place doesn't just feel empty:* **Marilyn** *has taken him at his word. Pictures gone, furniture. He walks from room to room as if in a trance. It is a bright winter's day and the light in the room is odd, unfamiliar. He goes into the kitchen/dining room. It is virtually bare. A lonely liquidiser on the table, the dresser denuded. He walks through to the sitting room where he and* **Marilyn** *had divided the records and books. It is particularly stark and actually quite elegant. He goes to the stereo and puts on Vivaldi's 'Stabat Mater'. He sits on the sofa, throws his head back. The music, the sunlight, flooding in.*


*The M4. A Saturday soon after. Early morning.*

*The Beetle pop-pops towards Bristol.* **Dominic** *is driving. The radio is on loud. He leaves the motorway and joins the road to Bristol.*

*Two girls are standing, hitching* **Angie** *and* **Stephanie**. *Marvellous women.* **Dominic** *stops to pick them up.*

**Dominic** Hello. Where d'you want to go?

**Stephanie** Bristol?

**Dominic** Great. Get in.

**Angie** *struggles to get into the back seat, the child seat is in her way.* **Stephanie** *sits in the front next to* **Dominic**.

**Dominic** So. Where can I take you? I don't actually know Bristol.

**Stephanie** Anywhere in the centre is fine thanks. (*Turns to* **Angie** *for confirmation.*) Yeah? (**Angie** *nods.*)

**Dominic** Okay. And what, are you up for the weekend?

**Stephanie** No, we live in Bristol . . . well Clifton.

**Dominic** Right.

**Stephanie** We went to a party in Bath. And it went on a bit. (*She laughs.*) Hence our party frocks.

*You wouldn't have known that* **Stephanie** *was in her party frock – not that she's dressed unattractively. It's just that she makes no concessions to High Street fashion or make-up.*

**Dominic** Right.

**Stephanie** How about you?

**Dominic** Oh, I haven't been to a party. (*To* **Angie**.) Are you okay in the back there? I think the seat unclips if you . . .

**Angie** I'm fine. You have a baby, don't you?

**Dominic** Yeah. I do.

**Angie** How old?

**Dominic** Oh. He's just over a year, I think.

**Angie** (*she likes babies*) Oh. What's his name?

**Dominic** Jack. What's Bristol like?

**Angie** Good.

**Stephanie** Good.

**Dominic** Are you students?

**Stephanie** I'm not.

**Angie**  I am.

**Dominic**  (*to* **Stephanie**)  What do you do?

**Stephanie**  (*enthusiastically*)  Well, I was a student. This is my first job, actually. I'm working at a women's advisory centre. It's great.

**Dominic**  It sounds great. Do they have a men's advisory centre?

**Stephanie**  (*smiling but cool*)  No. I don't think so.

**Angie**  (*diplomatically*)  I'm doing teacher training.

**Dominic**  Ah, you enjoying it?

**Angie**  Yeah.

**Stephanie**  (*to* **Dominic**)  What do you do?

**Dominic**  Oh, I'm an entirely frivolous person. Uh, at the moment . . . What am I doing? Uh, I think I'm doing 'O' level life.

**Stephanie**  Is that a full-time job?

**Dominic**  Seems to be.

**Stephanie**  So you're unwaged, then?

**Dominic**  No, uh, I get a grant.

**Stephanie**  Do you not like talking about yourself?

**Dominic**  (*thrown*)  Uh. I don't mind.

**Stephanie**  It's up to you. Anyway the music's good.

**Dominic**  Uh. What I'm doing . . . Well, my wife's just left me and moved here and I'm going to see my son. For the first time.

*The girls don't know what to say.* **Dominic** *turns up the music.*

*Bristol.* **Philip**'s *new shop. A little later.*

**Dominic** *has dropped off the girls and found* **Philip**'s *shop.*

*The shop is not open yet.* **Dominic** *peers through the window. His view is restricted by a venetian blind, but he can see* **Philip** *working with a saw. It is shambolic, but has the makings of a smart place. Tasteful restoration.*

**Marilyn** *comes in with a mug of tea for* **Philip**. *She has* **Jack** *plaited into one arm. They talk. It's inaudible through the glass, but clearly they're close. They kiss. For a second,* **Dominic** *is presented with a tableau of* *radiant family life:* **Philip**, **Marilyn**, **Jack**. *Then* **Marilyn** *glances at the window and sees* **Dominic**.

*Bristol. The same afternoon.*

**Dominic** *and* **Jack**'s *afternoon is a melancholy exploration of Bristol's public amenities. The highlight is the zoo.* **Jack** *is largely unimpressed. Then there's a push in the pushchair. A drive in the car. A visit to a newsagent's. And to the park, where* **Jack** *stays in his buggy, and* **Dominic** *sits on a bench. In the course of the afternoon,* **Jack** *is changed several times.*

**Philip**'s *new flat. Simultaneously.*

**Philip** *comes in to find* **Marilyn** *sitting – morose – in the middle of a half-decorated room.*

**Philip** (*gently*) You offered to make me a cup of tea an hour ago. (*She doesn't respond.*) Can I get you one?

**Marilyn** What would you do with a baby in a city you didn't know?

**Philip** He could have stayed here.

**Marilyn** Would you?

**Philip** I don't know. I'd go to an information centre. I don't know. Do you think there's more we could do?

**Marilyn** Probably not.

**Philip** Dominic's not short on ingenuity. This is the first time. He's bound to feel . . .

**Marilyn** What about Jack? He was crying when they left. Oh and how many times can you patrol the same places? It's no fun for him.

**Philip** Well that's true whoever takes him.

**Marilyn** (*harshly*) Don't keep on having a reply please Philip.

**Philip** Okay.

*He walks out of the room.* **Marilyn**, *repentant, goes after him.*

**Marilyn** Philip. I'm sorry. (*She reaches out to him.*)

**Philip** (*the rebuke is forgotten*) Do you want that cup of tea?

**Marilyn** *nods*.


*Outside. The same afternoon.*

*Roaming aimlessly.* **Dominic** *and* **Jack** *while away their afternoon.*
**Dominic** *struggles to change* **Jack** *in the back of the Beetle.*


**Philip**'s *flat. Late afternoon.*

**Marilyn** *is lying on* **Philip**'s *lap upstairs on the couch. The doorbell rings.*

**Philip** I'll let them in.

**Marilyn** No, it's okay. I'll go.

**Marilyn** *goes down and opens the door to* **Dominic** *and* **Jack**. *Mother and son practically grab each other.* **Dominic** *parks the buggy.* **Marilyn**, *feeling* **Jack**, *notices that he needs changing.*

**Marilyn** Hello!

**Dominic** (*ferociously cheerful*) Say 'Hi, Mum.'

**Marilyn** Are you all right? Did you have a nice afternoon?

**Dominic** Yeah great!

**Marilyn** Was he okay?

**Dominic** Yeah. We met a few people. We took in a movie. Played pool.

**Marilyn** (*to* **Jack**) You look tired, darling.

**Dominic** I think he is. All that fresh air.

**Marilyn** Will you come in? There's food.

**Dominic** No. I want to get back. While there's still some daylight.

**Marilyn** Okay. (*Pauses.*) So.

**Dominic** So.

**Marilyn** Next weekend?

**Dominic** Great.

**Marilyn** Did he sleep at all?

**Dominic**  Not really.

**Marilyn**  And you found the park?

**Dominic**  Yeah.

**Marilyn**  Yeah . . . So.

**Dominic**  (*to* **Jack**)  Well, bye-bye then.

**Marilyn**  Say 'Bye, Dad. Thanks for a nice afternoon'.

**Dominic**  (*in exaggerated tones, as if talking to the baby*)  We had a milk shake.

**Marilyn**  (*in similar tones*)  Did you! (*Pause, nothing else to say.*)  Okay.

**Dominic**  Right . . . well I'll see you . . . next week.

**Marilyn**  All right. Drive safely. (**Dominic** *goes to the car. To* **Jack**.) Say 'Bye'.

**Marilyn** *shuts the door. She carries* **Jack** *upstairs to* **Philip**. **Philip** *has picked up on the decorating. He looks round inquiringly.*

**Philip**  Okay?

**Marilyn**  (*exasperated, tearful, of* **Jack** )  He's soaked, Philip.


**Dominic**'s *house. Sitting room. That night.*

**Chris** *and* **Dominic** *loll about on the floor. The television is on. Snooker. There's a bottle of wine, cutlery and glasses.* **Siobhan** *comes in with a tray full of steaming goodies.*

**Chris**  Mmm!

**Dominic**  Siobhan – you're great!

**Siobhan**  I know.

**Dominic**  You don't know how welcome this is. I'm exhausted.

**Siobhan**  Well, shut up and eat. And then I want to hear all about your day.

**Chris**  (*jovially*)  Christ. Dom, I thought you'd got away from this!

**Siobhan**  You can shut up, too. And does anybody mind if I change this? There's a film on the other side.

**Chris**  (*enjoying himself*)  Bloody hell.

*She changes channel. They dig in happily.*

**Philip**'s *new flat. The same night. Very late.*

**Jack**'s *room.* **Marilyn** *is holding* **Jack**, *trying to soothe him back to sleep.* **Philip** *appears sleepily, wearing pyjamas.*

**Philip**  No luck?

**Marilyn**  No. It's hopeless. He goes to sleep, I put him down, and he wakes up. He's really upset.

**Philip**  Do you want me to have a go?

**Marilyn**  No. It's all right.

**Philip**  Why don't you bring him to bed?

**Marilyn**  I think I'll have to.

**Philip**  Come on, then.

**Marilyn**  I feel like I'm sleepwalking.

*All three go through to* **Philip/Marilyn**'s *bed and get in.* **Jack** *in the middle. He doesn't stop crying. He won't lie down.*

**Marilyn**  (*despairing*)  Jack. Come on!

**Dominic**'s *house. The same night.*

*The bedroom. It's fairly empty. There's a futon rolled up in one corner.* **Siobhan** *and* **Dominic** *enter, holding hands. They survey the room.*

**Siobhan**  It's pretty austere.

**Dominic**  Oh, yes.

**Siobhan**  (*realising why it seems so bare*)  Dom. Where's the bed?

**Dominic** *unravels the futon with an impressive flourish.*

**Siobhan**  Dominic, you're so trendy!

**Dominic**  Yeah.

**Siobhan**  Are you drunk?

**Dominic**  Yeah.

**Siobhan**  Because this feels sort of romantic.

**Dominic**  Yeah.

*They kiss.* **Dominic** *goes to the wardrobe and pulls out the duvet stuffed inside it. Then envelops himself and* **Siobhan** *in it. The headless creature* *they have created moves silently to the futon and descends onto it. There's a bit of wriggling and fumbling and then **Dominic**'s head appears. He gets up.*

**Siobhan** (*apprehensive*)  Now what?

**Dominic**  I forgot the sheet.

*He fetches the sheet from the wardrobe. In a complicated movement, he rolls **Siobhan** and the duvet over to one side of the futon, covers the exposed half of the futon with the sheet, then rolls **Siobhan** and the duvet back to the other side, and covers the second half with the rest of the sheet. It's a remarkably slick operation. He gets in and pulls the duvet over them.*

*Bristol streets. A week later. Early afternoon.*

**Dominic** *pushing* **Jack** *along in the buggy. They pass a launderette.* **Angie**'s *sitting inside.* **Dominic** *double takes. Stops, and bangs on the window.* **Angie** *looks up, registers who it is.* **Dominic** *waves. She comes out.*

**Dominic**  Hello!

**Angie**  Hello.

**Dominic**  This is the boy – Jack!

**Angie** (*to* **Jack**)  Hello! (*Looks at* **Dominic**.) Coincidence.

**Dominic**  Yeah.

**Angie**  I thought about you last weekend. We both did. We wondered how you managed.

**Dominic**  Well thank you. We survived. (*To* **Jack**.) Didn't we, eh? (**Jack** *doesn't respond. To* **Angie**.) Nothing. He's sulking.

**Angie**  Oh. Why?

**Dominic**  No idea. He won't say. How's teaching?

**Angie** (*correcting*)  Learning to teach.

**Dominic**  Right.

**Angie**  It's fine. I thought you might not have remembered.

**Dominic**  Oh, I remembered. Look, uh, are you by yourself?

**Angie**  Yeah. Well, I'm with my laundry.

**Dominic**  Well, we were thinking of having a cup of coffee. So do you want to come along?

**Angie**  Okay.

**Dominic**  Great.

**Angie**  (*she points in the direction* **Dominic** *and* **Jack** *have just been*)  There's one that way.

**Dominic**  Is there?

**Angie**  Yeah.

**Dominic**  (*to* **Jack**)  Oi! We missed it! (*To* **Angie**.)  Look, uh, look . . . I don't know your name.

**Angie**  Angie.

**Dominic**  I'm Dominic. Hello Angie.

**Angie**  Hello. So what did you do last week?

**Dominic**  Oh. Anything I could think of, really. I resorted to everything except sweets.

**Angie**  (*laughing*)  Why not sweets? Are you against sweets?

**Dominic**  No. Not at all. No.

**Angie**  Well, you should be. If he doesn't eat sweets now, he won't want to when he's older.

**Dominic**  Is that so? Well, I'm afraid I can't monitor his diet quite so closely. But anyway, not sweets because somebody I know didn't live with her father and he used to take her out at weekends and every evening after those outings she'd be really sick from chocolate and candy floss and anything else he could cram down to keep her happy.

**Angie**  Oh dear.

**Dominic**  Exactly.

**Angie**  So, it was parks and swings and walks and . . .?

**Dominic**  Yes. All that. And a cafe and the zoo – he likes the zoo – and, uh, I can't think . . .

**Angie**  Where will you go if it's raining?

**Dominic**  Everybody asks me that.

**Angie**  (*of* **Jack**)  He lives near here, doesn't he?

**Dominic**  Yes, that's right. Yeah, a couple of streets away.

**Angie** It's just that . . . well, so do we, and you'd be welcome to come round if you wanted. Well, if you were at a loose end. In fact, why not come now and I'll make you coffee. Steph will be really pleased to see both of you.

**Dominic** Steph's your mate, right?

**Angie** Yeah.

**Dominic** Well thank you. Great. (*To* **Jack**.) That's good, isn't it?

**Angie** He's still sulking.

**Dominic** Yep.

**Angie** Don't let me forget my laundry. Oh, what am I doing! It's this way!

*They turn round and go back the way they were coming, another little family in the making.*

# Part Three

**Dominic**'s *house. Morning.*

*A Saturday morning some weeks on. The ritual drive to Bristol is now established.* **Dominic** *is always late. Today is no exception: he hurtles out of the house, putting on his jacket as he goes, holding his toast with his teeth. He is starting the car and already has the stereo up impossibly loud, when* **Siobhan** *hurtles out after him. She is bare-footed, and wearing a coat over not much else. She's carrying a bag.*

**Siobhan** Dom! Dom!

*She gets to the car just as he is about to pull away.* **Dominic** *sees her, winds down his window and turns off the music.*

**Dominic** Hi. (*Apologising for not having said goodbye.*) Sorry, but I'm late and I didn't want to wake you.

**Siobhan** I know, but you forgot the present for Jack. (*She hands him the bag.*)

**Dominic** Thanks. You should give it to him yourself. It's a shame.

**Siobhan** I know.

**Dominic** I'll try and bring him back for a weekend soon.

**Siobhan** I'd like that.

**Dominic** So would I Siobhan. Anyway . . . (*He makes a weary gesture: the long journey ahead of him.*) See you tomorrow.

**Siobhan** Don't go back to sleep.

**Dominic** *turns on the stereo again. Loud.*

**Dominic** Infallible.

**Siobhan** I may still be here when you get back. My feet are frozen to the pavement.

**Dominic** (*unable to hear*) What?

**Siobhan** (*shouting over the music*) My feet are frozen!

**Dominic** Oh. Sorry. (*He leans out, and they kiss fleetingly before he drives off.*)

**Siobhan** *watches him drive off.*

*Outside **Chris**'s house. A few minutes later.*

*The VW stops outside **Chris**'s house, it's arrival heralded by the stereo.*
***Dominic** beep-beeps to the waiting and impatient **Chris**. **Chris** hops in,*
*and they set off to Bristol.*

*The VW en-route to Bristol. A little later. **Dominic** is filling **Chris** in with*
*the complex upheavals of his new life as a single man.*

**Dominic**  I'm in love, Chris.

**Chris**  Well thank God for that. 'Cos the sackcloth and ashes
routine was getting to be a right pain.

**Dominic**  Do you like the name Celia?

**Chris**  It's all right.

**Dominic**  She's so beautiful. I mean, I don't know anything about
her, but she's so beautiful.

**Chris** (*unimpressed*)  Yeah. You said.

**Dominic**  No, really. And she's so unimpressed. You know she's just
. . . Totally. Totally unimpressed.

**Chris**  Like Marilyn, you mean?

**Dominic**  You know what I mean.

**Chris**  No. I don't. I mean Siobhan's very impressed. Settle for that.
I would.

**Dominic**  Well, you couldn't bullshit Celia. You just couldn't.

**Chris**  Yeah, well I've never been able to bullshit any women. They
just say, 'That's bullshit Chris'.

**Dominic**  No, I really want you to meet her, Chris. You know she's
made a film about Rothko?

**Chris** (*unsure who Rothko is*)  Is that good?

**Dominic**  Yeah. I think so. (*Pause. Then excited.*) Oh yeah, she takes
these photographs . . . You know, it's the first time I've looked at a
picture of myself and thought yes, that's me, that's what I look like.

**Chris** (*unexcited*)  I've never had that problem, either.

**Dominic**  But the thing is: what about Angie?

**Chris** (*struggling to keep track*)  This is Angie we're going to see in
Bristol?

**Dominic** (*thinking of **Angie** now*)  She's lovely.

**Chris** You know, you're like a big kid who's just discovered what his willie's for.

**Dominic** (*not listening still thinking of* **Angie**) It's all very strange, Chris. What's happening. If we stayed at Angie's tonight would that bother you?

**Chris** (*boggled*) Yes!

**Dominic** Well . . . Celia's just sort of hypothetical. I've got high hopes for you and Stephanie.

**Chris** (*completely confused*) Stephanie.

**Dominic** Stephanie's great.

*They drive on.*

*The swimming baths. The same time.*

**Philip**, **Marilyn** and **Jack** *are in the learner's pool of a busy swimming baths.* **Philip**, *holding* **Jack**, *spins round in circles, swooshing the baby in the water. He makes aeroplane noises.* **Jack** *loves it.* **Marilyn** *looks concerned though, and after the spin she takes* **Jack** *from* **Philip**.

**Marilyn** (*to* **Philip**.) You're putting on weight.

**Philip** (*inspecting himself*) I'm middle-aged. It's allowed.

**Marilyn** No it's not.

**Philip** Shut up, I bite.

*He ducks playfully under the surface, perhaps to bite. In the process* **Jack** *is disturbed.*

**Marilyn** Careful, Philip. Gently! (**Jack** *beings to cry.*) You are stupid. Now look what you've done.

**Philip** (*weary of all this over protectiveness*) Oh God.

**Jack** *screams.* **Philip** *leaves* **Marilyn** *and the baby, and heads for the deep end.*

*The coffee bar overlooking the pool. A little later.*

**Philip** *is sitting, still a little sore from the pool episode, drinking tea.* **Marilyn** *arrives holding* **Jack**. *She's fretful.*

**Philip** Okay?

**Marilyn** I think we'd better go. I don't want to be out when Dominic arrives.

**Philip** There's plenty of time. Have a drink.

**Marilyn** Why did you go off like that?

**Philip** I wish you'd relax about Jack. He loves the water. He's fearless.

**Marilyn** Only because I've never given him anything to be frightened about.

**Philip** No.

**Marilyn** Well, yes.

**Philip** Why are you taking it out on me?

**Marilyn** What do you mean?

**Philip** I will not be banged over the head every single day with Dominic's pain.

**Marilyn** Can we just go to the car, please?

**Philip** *drinks his tea.*

**Marilyn** (*insistent*) Please?

**Philip** In a minute.

**Marilyn** Can we go to the car *now?*

**Philip** When I've finished my tea.

**Marilyn** I'll see you there.

*She is angry. She turns and leaves.*

*Bristol. The same time.*

**Dominic** *and* **Chris**, *in the VW, are approaching* **Stephanie** *and* **Angie** *'s house.*

**Dominic** I hate this journey. I'm always late. I hate the whole day, the whole thing.

**Chris** What? Seeing Jack?

**Dominic**  No. Not Jack. No. The bits around him. I don't think it's him.

**Chris**  How's Marilyn with you?

**Dominic**  Okay. Cool. A bit closed. I don't know.

**Chris**  (*facetious*)  Just the same as usual then.

**Dominic**  We're almost there.

**Chris**  Well, don't go maudlin on me. I thought you said these women were marvellous.

**Dominic**  They are. (**Dominic** *spots* **Stephanie** *parking her bike as they pull up outside the house.*) There's Steph.

**Dominic** *beep-beeps.*


*The swimming baths. A staircase.*

**Philip**, *coming down, meets a repentant* **Marilyn** *returning.* **Jack** *is in her arms.*

**Philip**  Sorry. I was coming.

**Marilyn**  No, *I'm* sorry. We were coming back. Besides, it's earlier than I thought. I want a drink. (*She nods to* **Jack**.) And so does he. Is that allowed?

**Philip**  (*smiling*)  Yeah.

*With* **Jack** *squashed between them, they try to embrace. Then they turn to go back to the cafe.*

**Marilyn**  Philip, just a minute. (*They stop.*) I think I might be pregnant.

**Philip**  Oh.

**Marilyn**  Exactly. It's just, I feel like I am. And I'm very late. I'm hoping it's just anxiety. But I'm anxious because I don't think it is.

**Philip**  Then tonight can be a celebration. (*They have planned to go out while* **Philip**'s *sister baby-sits.*)

**Marilyn**  Would you celebrate?

**Philip**  (*smiles*)  Yes.

**Marilyn**  Philip –

**Philip** (*carrying on for her*) But do we have to go out tonight? (*Smiles.*) Not if you're that worried about it. But you needn't be. Katherine's wonderful with kids. She practically brought me up. Come on, let's get you two a drink.

*They move off, again, towards the cafe.*

**Angie** *and* **Stephanie** *'s house. A little later.*

**Stephanie** *escorts the boys into the living room.*

**Stephanie** Come on in. (*They remain standing.* **Dominic** *is anxious to get going.*) Well, sit yourselves down.

*They do so. But* **Angie** *comes in, brushing her hair, and* **Dominic** *gets up to kiss her.*

**Dominic** Hello. How are you?

**Angie** Okay. I was washing my hair.

**Dominic** Fine. (*The time, not the hair.*)

**Angie** Although I've been up for ages, eh Steph?

**Stephanie** Hours. This is Chris.

**Angie** Hello Chris.

**Chris** Hi. I'm surprised we were allowed in, actually.

**Stephanie** (*explains, cheerfully*) I think I was rude and I'm sorry. It's just habit.

**Angie** Ignore her. Underneath the teeth she's all heart.

**Stephanie** All bust actually. But underneath that, definitely.

**Chris** Well, good.

**Dominic** He's almost speechless. That's a record.

**Chris** No, it's just that I'm used to women more sort of . . .

**Stephanie** (*sharp*) More sort of what?

**Chris** (*looks to* **Dominic** *in the hope of being bailed out*) I wish I hadn't started this. (*To* **Dominic**.) Look, I'll wait in the car, shall I?

**Dominic** No, no. I want you to stay here while I go and pick up Jack.

**Angie** There's no need. I'm ready now, Dom. We can go straight to the park.

**Dominic** Ah well, I'd like to pick him up on my own if that's all right.

**Angie** Yes, of course.

**Dominic** (*not entirely honest*) It's just that he might be overwhelmed – by so many faces.

**Angie** Do you want a cup of coffee before you go?

**Dominic** Look, I'd love one but I'm already late actually. I'll see you all later, okay?

**Angie** I'll see you out.

**Dominic** *and* **Angie** *go out, leaving* **Chris** *and* **Stephanie** *alone.*

**Chris** (*referring to the incident on the way into the house*) I think what I really meant was that everything Dominic said about you was absolutely true. (*This is a compliment.*)

**Stephanie** (*affected archness*) Really? What was that?

**Angie** (*returning from seeing* **Dominic** *out*) Do you want a coffee, Chris?

**Chris** Uh, yes please. Thank you.

**Angie** Okay.

*She leaves. A beat.*

**Chris** Very nice things.

**Stephanie** I'm sorry?

**Chris** What Dominic said about you.

*They're both quite shy now.*

**Stephanie** (*laughs*) Oh right. (*Pause.*) Ditto.

**Chris** What?

**Stephanie** The things he said about you. Ditto.

**Chris** (*suddenly understanding*) Oh! Ditto! Right. (*He says it quietly to himself.*) Ditto.

**Marilyn/Philip** *'s flat. A little later.*

*The flat has its own access, separate from the shop.* **Marilyn** *opens the door* *to* **Dominic**.

**Dominic** Sorry. There was traffic. I was going to call.

**Marilyn** Will you next time? I was getting worried. It's almost midday.

**Dominic** (*echoing the 'almost'*) Well it's almost 120 miles. I'm not that late.

**Marilyn** I don't know why you don't take the train.

**Dominic** Then you could have the car.

**Marilyn** I do actually think I need it more than you. Anyway . . .

*She is anxious to get the acrimony over before they go inside – so that* **Philip***'s sister doesn't see it.*

**Dominic** *is anxious to get in, get* **Jack** *and get going.*

**Dominic** Anyway. What's Jack doing?

**Marilyn** He's upstairs with Katherine.

**Dominic** Who's Katherine?

**Marilyn** Oh, Philip's sister. She's staying for a few days.

**Dominic** How is he?

**Marilyn** He's fine. He's not sleeping. But he's fine. So, are you going to eat here or out?

**Dominic** Out. (*Pause.*) How are you?

**Marilyn** Oh I'm fine. I haven't got a job. I don't go out. I don't know anyone. But that's my choice, so I can't complain, can I?

**Dominic** No. I guess not.

**Marilyn** Oh . . . (*A big event.*) Jack is walking. (*She smiles.*)

**Dominic** (*this hurts, but he covers it*) He's not! (**Marilyn** *nods, smiling.*) Really!

**Marilyn** He took a few steps on Wednesday.

**Dominic** (*reflectively*) Wow!

**Dominic** *is utterly deflated.*

**Marilyn** So, what are you going to do today?

**Dominic** Oh, I don't know. Usual stuff.

**Marilyn** Will you try not to let him sleep in the afternoon? It makes the evening impossible.

**Dominic** (*stung*) I don't want him to sleep either, you know. It's the only chance I get to see him. But it's hard just to wake him up.

**Marilyn** Well I have to.

**Dominic** Shall we just go and see what he's up to?

**Marilyn** Okay.

**Dominic** Incidentally, my parents were asking if there was any possibility of my taking him there for a day? (*Pause.*) They haven't seen him for so long, that's all.

**Marilyn** Okay.

**Dominic** I said it was early days. But – eventually.

**Marilyn** (*nodding*) No, right.

*They turn and rather mournfully go in.*

*Upstairs,* **Katherine** *is holding* **Jack**.

**Marilyn** Katherine, this is Dominic.

**Katherine** (*awkward*) Hello.

**Dominic** (*awkward*) Hi. You're Philip's sister.

**Katherine** Yes, that's right.

**Marilyn** I'll get his things. (*Goes out to get* **Jack***'s things.*)

*There's a pause. Then* **Katherine** *gives* **Jack** *to* **Dominic**.

**Dominic** (*to* **Jack**) Hello. Hello.

**Katherine** He's lovely.

**Dominic** Yes.

*Outside* **Philip** *'s shop. A minute or two later.*

**Dominic** *makes his way with* **Jack** *and paraphernalia to the car.* **Dominic** *is not very happy.*

**Dominic** (*as they struggle into the car*) So you're walking now, are you? Well you just make damn sure you do these things on Saturdays? Okay? Okay? (**Dominic** *gets the present from* **Siobhan**, *which is on the back seat.*) And this is for you. It's from your Auntie

Siobhan. Let's have a look. (**Dominic** *opens the present. It is a tiny fisherman's smock. He holds it up against* **Jack**.) Pretty stylish, huh? I might wear it after you.

*He straps* **Jack** *into his seat.*

*The zoo. Later that afternoon.*

**Dominic** *and* **Chris** *sit on a bench. As they talk, they watch* **Angie**, **Stephanie** *and* **Jack** *who are wholeheartedly enjoying the zoo.*

**Dominic**  What do you think of Steph?

**Chris**  She's great.

**Dominic**  Pack in the typing classes. Join the Women's Movement.

**Chris**  I think she'd eat me.

**Dominic**  Be fun, though, eh?

**Chris**  Angie's beautiful.

**Dominic**  Yeah. Jack loves her.

**Chris**  And I think you'd eat *her*. (*Pause.*) Stephanie asked me if you were seeing anyone else.

**Dominic**  What did you say?

**Chris**  I said: 'Huh?'

**Dominic**  How did that go down?

**Chris**  Not great.

**Angie** *and* **Stephanie** *are having fun. They shout over to* **Dominic** *and* **Chris**.

**Angie**  Come on! Look at this.

**Dominic** *and* **Chris** *get up and go to see what the fuss is all about.*

**Stephanie**  Come on! What have you two been nattering about?

**Philip**'s *shop. Later that day.*

**Dominic** *is returning* **Jack** *after their day out.* **Marilyn** *and* **Dominic** *stand at the door as they talk. There are several bags at their feet:* **Jack**'s *things from the car.*

**Marilyn**  Nice day?

**Dominic**  Yeah.

**Marilyn**  I'm sorry about earlier. I was . . .

**Dominic**  I'm sorry I was late.

**Marilyn**  Did he walk for you?

**Dominic**  Yeah. Incredible.

**Marilyn**  I know. (*To* **Jack**, *who is wearing the smock from* **Siobhan**.) I like this. Where did it come from?

**Dominic**  It's great, isn't it. I got it at home.

**Marilyn**  It's lovely. So. Did he sleep at all?

**Dominic**  A bit.

**Marilyn**  I hope he'll sleep a bit tonight as well.

**Dominic**  So do I.

**Dominic** *gives* **Jack** *to* **Marilyn**.

**Marilyn**  You going straight back?

**Dominic**  Yeah. I expect so. Do some work. Are you doing anything interesting?

**Marilyn**  (*meaning no*)  What do you think?

**Dominic**  Listen, about the car –

**Marilyn**  It's okay.

**Dominic**  No, I was thinking – perhaps we could work something out.

**Marilyn**  Okay. Anyway. (*To* **Jack**, *whom she is feeling with concern*.) You're a bit wet, aren't you? Come on and let's get you changed.

**Dominic**  (*hurt by the implication*)  I do change him, you know. He's had four clean nappies today: the last about an hour ago.

**Marilyn**  Right.

**Dominic**  I'll keep the wrappers in future.

**Marilyn**  I believe you.

*A pause.* **Dominic** *decides to let it go.*

**Dominic** (*to* **Jack**)  Bye-bye, darling. See you next weekend.

**Marilyn**  Say, 'Bye Dominic, thanks for a nice day.'

**Dominic** (*stung*)  Is that what he's going to call me? Dominic?

**Marilyn**  Why? What do you want him to call you?

**Dominic** (*incredulous, aggressive, bitter*)  How about Daddy?

*A pause. The point is not lost on* **Marilyn**. *She cannot answer.*

**Dominic**  Anyway. I'll see you Marilyn.

*He quickly turns, gets into the car and leaves. The emphasis on 'Marilyn' hanging unpleasantly behind him. She watches him drive off* **Jack**, *soaking, in her arms.* **Philip** *emerges from the shop. He says nothing, but starts picking up the debris to carry indoors.*

*A Chinese Restaurant. Later the same evening.*

*The restaurant is crowded.* **Chris** *and* **Dominic**, **Stephanie** *and* **Angie** *– the girls changed, the boys scrubbed – are squashed into a booth where they prepare to eat.* **Dominic** *is distracted, depressed.*

**Chris** (*to* **Dominic**.) Hey.

**Dominic**  What?

**Chris**  Exactly. What?

**Dominic**  I'm sorry. I'm tired. Long day. (*Leans over to the girls.*) How are you two?

**Angie**  Fine.

**Stephanie**  Fine thanks, dad. Can we play again next weekend?

**Dominic** (*not joining in*)  I expect so.

**Chris**  Now listen, when this food arrives, there are to be no knives and forks. Agreed?

**Angie**  Well . . . I can't use chopsticks.

**Chris**  Nor can I. Can you, Dom?

**Dominic**  No. Not really.

**Stephanie**  I can knit. That's similar.

**Angie**  I can knit.

**Chris** Well, there you are then: you two have got an advantage before we even start. (*Thinks.*) Although I fail to see what knitting's got to do with it.

**Stephanie** (*doubtfully*) Two long thin things.

**Chris** No, look, my theory is if none of us can do it, there's no problem. Because then we can all learn together without somebody scoffing the lot.

**Stephanie** But I'm starving!

**Chris** (*enjoying himself*) Well, there's your incentive, then.

**Stephanie** Okay.

**Angie** Okay.

**Chris** (*to* **Dominic**) Okay?

**Dominic** Yeah.

**Chris** Good-o.


**Marilyn** *and* **Philip** *come into the restaurant, dressed up. A celebration, but also intimate, romantic.*

**Marilyn** Do you think I should just ring Katherine to see if she's all right?

**Philip** No. I don't. I've given her the number. What I think you *should* do, is relax.

*They are seated by a polite but fantastically busy waiter. They don't see* **Dominic**'s *table.*

**Marilyn** (*opening the menu*) I'd forgotten what it's like to be out.

**Philip** You look wonderful.

**Marilyn** I feel ancient.

**Philip** You *are* ancient.

**Marilyn** (*relaxing*) Well, thank you. (*She laughs.*)

**Philip** Will you marry me?

**Marilyn** No, I'm married already.

**Philip** But apart from that?

**Marilyn** Why?

**Philip** Because I want you to marry me.

**Marilyn** But why marriage?

**Philip** Why not?

**Marilyn** Why repeat something that both of us have got wrong before?

**Philip** Well, what if you are pregnant?

*There are squeals of laughter from* **Dominic**'s *table. The chopsticks have become the source of great hilarity.* **Philip** *looks over briefly. Double-takes.*

**Philip** Isn't that Chris Caldwell? And Dominic?

*At the same time, something makes* **Dominic** *look over at* **Marilyn** *and* **Philip**'s *table. He double-takes. Freezes. Without thinking, he puts down his chopsticks and picks up a fork. Prods his food.*

**Marilyn** (*quickly*) Philip, I want to go.

**Chris** (*following* **Dominic**'s *stare*) Dominic –

**Dominic** She said she never went out.

**Angie** (*still playing the chopsticks game*) Dom! You're cheating!

**Dominic** Yeah.

**Stephanie** What's going on?

**Chris** Are you going to go over?

**Dominic** No. I want to leave, actually. Does anybody mind?

*The girls don't know what's going on.*

**Stephanie** Yes we do!

**Dominic** Well, why don't you three finish the meal? I'll meet you outside or something.

**Angie** (*concerned*) I'll come with you, Dom.

**Dominic** No. Please. (*The last thing he wants* **Marilyn** *to see.*) Really, you eat. (*He gets up from his seat.*)

**Chris** They're going.

**Dominic** Oh shit.

**Dominic** *and* **Chris** *watch as* **Marilyn** *and* **Philip** *leave.* **Philip** *mutters something to the waiter (who's come to take their order) as they go. They don't acknowledge* **Dominic** *or* **Chris**.

**Dominic** Shit.

**Dominic**'s *bedroom. Saturday morning, a week later.*

*The bedroom is still spartan (as is the whole house.)* **Dominic** *is rather cultivating the austerity look.* **Dominic** *and* **Siobhan** *are in bed. (The futon.) He opens an eye and checks his watch. He's overslept. He curses, then unravels himself elaborately from the sleeping* **Siobhan**. *He hunts for clothes, noisily.* **Siobhan** *stirs.*

**Siobhan**  What time is it?

**Dominic**  Late.

**Siobhan**  Oh.

**Dominic**  (*annoyed*)  Yeah: oh.

**Siobhan**  What time should you be there?

**Dominic**  Now. I don't know. Basically now.

**Siobhan**  (*suddenly enthusiastic*)  Hey. I'd quite like to come. Could I?

**Dominic**  That would be nice, but I really have to go now.

**Siobhan**  I could be ready in a couple of minutes.

**Dominic**  (*pulling on some trousers*)  No. It's more than that, it's like . . . (*He turns and explains gravely.*)  It's not a good thing, these visits. I don't feel good about them. Also I want to have a clear time with the baby, I don't know, uncluttered.

**Siobhan**  (*dropping it*)  Okay.

**Dominic**  Do you know what I mean, though?

**Siobhan**  Sure.

**Dominic**  It's already confusing for him without . . . (*He trails off.*) Whatever.

**Siobhan**  Yes.

**Dominic**  I mean, obviously, at some stage. I for one would like the company. If only for the drive. Look, I have to go now, I'm sorry. (*He kisses her.*)

**Siobhan**  See you tonight.

**Dominic**  (*thrown*)  Uh. Well . . . I was thinking I might possibly stop over. Look, why don't we say if I'm back I'll come over to you?

**Siobhan**  (*smiles*)  Okay. Let's say that.

**Dominic** Okay. Go back to sleep now.

**Siobhan** Drive carefully.

**Dominic** Thanks.

*He pecks her again, and dashes out.* **Siobhan** *lies back in the bed. She's unhappy.*

**Marilyn/Philip**'s *bedroom. The same morning.*

**Marilyn**, **Philip** *and* **Jack** *are in bed, all squashed up.* **Philip** *has made some toast and stuff. He reads a novel,* **Jack** *plays,* **Marilyn** *muses.*

**Marilyn** Are you sure you don't mind?

**Philip** That's a trick question.

**Marilyn** How come?

**Philip** (*cheerfully*) Well, can a man safely mind his woman going to a women's conference?

**Marilyn** (*cheerfully*) *His* woman?

**Philip** Shut up. Anyway I don't. I'd like to go myself.

**Marilyn** Well you can't, can he Jack?

**Philip** What I'm really sore about is that I'll miss an hour in bed *by ourselves* this afternoon. (*To* **Jack**.) By ourselves! (*To* **Marilyn**.) Remember that curious sensation?

**Marilyn** You tell him to sod off, Jack. You came first.

**Philip** Well I hope you're not pregnant. The mind boggles.

**Marilyn** The family bed!

**Philip** Ugh! I'll go and sleep in the cot.

**Marilyn** We could get another cot and both sleep in them, and they could come in our bed.

**Philip** Or better still, get a double cot.

**Marilyn** (*solemn*) You're sure you don't mind handing him over to Dominic?

**Philip** No, that's fine.

**Marilyn** I'd really have liked to have taken him with me.

**Philip** Why didn't you arrange that? Dominic could have come tomorrow.

**Marilyn** I don't want to be awkward.

**Philip** It's not being awkward to rearrange the day.

**Marilyn** Okay, well I don't want to be selfish then.

**Philip** Better to be selfish than to be self-righteous about losing out on what you really want.

**Marilyn** You think?

**Philip** Yes. I do.

**Marilyn** Anyway, it's important for Jack to have a routine. It's important for Dominic, too. (*Thinks.*) Do you think he's having a 'thing' with one of those girls?

**Philip** (*putting down his book*) Ah!

**Marilyn** What do you mean, 'ah'?

**Philip** The taboo subject.

**Marilyn** Not at all. Why do you say that?

**Philip** We see Dominic with some women a week ago and you never mention it. That seems to me to make it taboo.

**Marilyn** They were both too young, anyway.

**Philip** Why?

**Marilyn** I know which one it was. I know just what he goes in for.

**Philip** (*astonished*) God!

**Marilyn** It was the black one with the doe eyes. (*That's* **Angie**.)

**Philip** How do you know?

**Marilyn** Because I do. Of course, if we wait a month we can always find out from reading his bloody cartoon strip.

**Philip** Well, you're not black, and you certainly haven't got doe eyes.

**Marilyn** You can lose doe eyes.

**Philip** (*teasing*) Really?

**Marilyn** And you can shut up.

**Philip** I find it hard to think of you as ever having doe eyes.

**Marilyn**  Have you ever had *black* eyes?

**Philip**  Jack, bite your mother.

*They fight in bed, happily. Spilling the things.*

**Angie/Stephanie**'s *house. The same morning.*

*The bathroom.* **Angie**'s *inside, washing her hair.* **Stephanie**'s *outside.*

**Stephanie**  Can I come in?

**Angie**  Go away.

**Stephanie**  What are you doing?

**Angie**  I'm washing my hair.

**Stephanie**  Well, let me in. I'm dying for a pee.

**Angie**  Hang on. Sorry.

**Angie** *unlocks the door, and* **Stephanie** *rushes in and sits on the lavatory.* **Angie** *is leaning over the bath, rinsing her hair with a plastic shower attachment.*

**Stephanie**  Do you have to wash your hair every Saturday?

**Angie**  Yes.

**Stephanie**  I'm annoyed.

**Angie**  I know.

**Stephanie**  With both of you.

**Angie**  Yes.

**Stephanie**  Are you listening?

**Angie**  Yes. (*She turns off the water, turns and faces* **Stephanie**.) You're annoyed with both of us.

**Stephanie**  Come to the conference.

**Angie**  I'll come to the stuff tomorrow.

**Stephanie**  (*still sitting on the lavatory*)  No. You should come both days.

**Angie**  I don't know. Perhaps Dom'll want to bring Jack. Then we can all come.

**Stephanie**  It's not really for men.

**Angie**  Why not?

**Stephanie**  Because men have conferences all the time. Because they get opportunities to talk about these things together at their places of work. Women are partitioned. Why am I telling you this? You know why.

**Angie**  It says men can go.

**Stephanie**  (*correcting*)  It says men can go if they're going to the single parent session.

**Angie**  Well, he is a single parent.

**Stephanie**  Well, he isn't actually. Marilyn is.

**Angie**  Why do you call her Marilyn? You don't know her.

**Angie** *is upset, vulnerable. A pause.* **Stephanie** *flushes the lavatory.*

**Stephanie**  Angie.

**Angie**  What?

**Stephanie**  Why do you only see Dominic at weekends?

**Angie**  (*humiliated but stubborn*)  Because he probably sees somebody else.

**Stephanie**  Yes, he probably does.

**Angie**  So why should that stop me washing my hair?

**Stephanie**  What does he say about it?

**Angie**  Nothing.

**Stephanie**  Don't you ask?

**Angie**  There's no time.

**Stephanie**  You have sex with him. Isn't there time to talk?

**Angie**  (*quiet*)  No. (*She pours some conditioner and begins to massage it in.*)

**Stephanie**  That's why you should come. (*Pause.*) Angie. It would be really good for you. You could put what's happening to you in some kind of context. With other women.

**Angie**  What do you mean, 'what's happening to me'? I happen to it too. I want it to happen.

**Stephanie**  (*unconvinced*)  Do you?

**Angie** (*stubborn*) And to see Jack, yes. I do actually. I know what's happening.

**Stephanie** (*suddenly*) Is that my conditioner?

**Angie** Yeah.

**Stephanie** (*rushing over from the loo*) Give us it back! (*She grabs the shower attachment, and rinses **Angie**'s hair, laughing.*)

**Angie** (*shrieking, laughing*) Steph! Get off!

*They battle for a few seconds, and **Stephanie** gets as much of the spray as **Angie**. Then the moment is gone. **Stephanie** drops the shower attachment and gently rubs **Angie**'s back. They are close. **Angie** is weeping. **Stephanie** holds her.*

**Philip**'s flat. Midday, Saturday.

**Philip** *comes into the sitting room carrying **Jack**. He's pursued by a breathless, contrite **Dominic**.*

**Philip** Come in.

**Dominic** I'm late.

**Philip** It's okay.

**Dominic** I can't believe I'm this late again.

**Philip** Marilyn's not here.

**Dominic** Oh.

**Philip** She's gone to a conference. (*Not entirely honest.*) She waited but you –

**Dominic** Right. (**Dominic** *is sullen. Visibly uncomfortable.*) Lots of traffic.

**Dominic** *approaches **Philip**, and virtually pulls **Jack** out of his arms.*

**Dominic** (*to **Jack***) Hello.

**Philip** (*making an effort*) He's really growing up, isn't he? (*No response.*) Still not sleeping much, though. Has Marilyn said? But he's terrific.

**Dominic** (*aggressive*) I really don't want him to call you Daddy. You know? (*Pause. Nothing from **Philip**. **Dominic** is in a dangerous, violent mood.*) Are you going to get married?

**Philip** I've no idea.

**Dominic** Christ. Well, that's one thing to be said for my son growing up with you: I'm sure he'll be able to sell things.

**Philip** (*civil*) Do you need to take anything with you? A change of clothes.

**Dominic** (*mock civility*) We could always play squash again, Philip.

**Philip** I don't think so.

**Dominic** No, I don't think so, either.

**Dominic** *goes to leave.*

**Philip** What I do think is that maybe you feel you're the only. person who suffers.

**Dominic** (*turning, coming back in*) I'm sorry. I didn't know it hurt, living with my wife and with my child.

**Philip** I know you didn't.

**Dominic** (*slowly*) Well, if it's such a drag, Philip, send them back.

**Philip** They don't belong to anyone.

**Dominic** (*quiet, menacing*) Fuck off, Philip, please.

**Dominic** *leaves, clutching* **Jack**.

**Angie** *'s bedroom. The same afternoon.*

*The curtains are closed.* **Dominic**, *dressed only in trousers, eases himself into bed alongside the sleeping* **Angie**. *She wakes.* **Dominic** *is easy.* **Angie** *isn't.*

**Dominic** You fell asleep.

**Angie** Did I?

**Dominic** I've been travelling between the two of you. (*He means her and* **Jack**, *who is asleep in the sitting room.*) You both looked so peaceful.

**Angie** Is he still asleep?

**Dominic** Yes. I'll wake him. I just wanted a few minutes with you.

**Angie** I must go.

**Dominic** You're funny.

**Angie** I don't think I'm funny.

**Dominic** I didn't mean funny.

**Angie** Will you come with me?

**Dominic** I don't think the baby's into feminism just yet. He prefers the swings.

**Angie** There's an adventure playground there.

**Dominic** You go. (*Easy.*) We'll go to the park. It's no problem.

**Angie** I didn't say it was a problem. It would have been nice for me.

**Dominic** (*distracted suddenly, as if he heard* **Jack**) Hang on. (*Listens.*) Sorry, go on.

**Angie** I'll have to be applying for jobs soon.

**Dominic** Oh. Right. (*Wary, but covering it.*)

**Angie** (*carefully*) Is there any point in my applying for one near you?

**Dominic** Well I should have thought – with the shortage of jobs – you should just apply for the job rather than the place. (*Pause.*) So, obviously, if there's one near me . . . (*Pause.*) Is there one?

**Angie** I don't know. (*Pause. Bleakly.*) I really like you. Dominic. Do you know that.

**Dominic** Yes.

**Angie** And Jack.

**Dominic** I'm sorry. (*Pause.*) I'm sorry. (*He looks down.*)

**Angie** (*sitting up*) What for?

**Dominic** Would you rather we stopped coming?

**Angie** No.

**Dominic** *rolls onto his stomach.*

**Dominic** Do you know what I'd really like?

**Angie** What?

**Dominic** For you to lie on my back.

*A long pause. Then* **Angie** *lies on his back. She is naked.*

It's wonderful.

**Angie** Why do you like this?

**Dominic** I don't know. I feel . . . I like the weight. I feel protected. If you're a man, it's a really unusual position.

**Angie** I could hit you.

**Dominic** Yes. you could (*In that position.*)

**Angie** No, I mean I want to hit you.

**Dominic** Oh.

*She thumps his back. Really hard. It doesn't make her feel any better. She rolls off and stares into space.* **Dominic** *is startled.*

*The park. A little later.*

**Dominic** *pushes* **Jack** *on a swing. He sings to* **Jack**.

*A girl,* **Theresa**, *is playing at the next swing. She's nine or ten. Her younger brother is climbing the steps of the slide nearby. They're urchins, dirty, hard, cheeky, great.*

**Theresa** (*watching* **Dominic** *push* **Jack**) Where's his mum?

**Dominic** What?

**Theresa** You on the dole?

**Dominic** No. Why?

**Theresa** What's his name?

**Dominic** Jack. What's yours?

**Theresa** My dad looked after us when he was on the dole. I had to cook. He didn't know how. He thinks sausages is cooking. Can you cook?

**Dominic** No.

**Theresa** My name's Theresa. (*Nods in the direction of her brother and the slide.*) And he's Darren.

**Dominic** My name's Dominic.

**Theresa** There's a girl at our school called Dominic.

**Dominic** Well, there you go, eh? (*Pause.*) Boy at my school called Theresa.

**Theresa** Bet there wasn't.

**Dominic** There was actually.

**Theresa** You married?

**Dominic** Yep.

**Theresa** Where's your ring then?

**Dominic** Men don't wear wedding rings.

**Theresa** Yes they do.

**Dominic** Well, I don't wear a wedding ring because, uh, I don't live with Jack's mother any more.

**Theresa** (*unabashed*) What, you divorced?

**Dominic** No.

**Theresa** Gonna be?

**Dominic** (*not amused*) What are you going to do when you grow up? Psychiatry?

**Theresa** (*doesn't know the word*) No.

**Darren** (*coming over*) I can swing on this upside down.

**Theresa** No you can't. (*To* **Dominic**.) Shall I push him?

**Dominic** Okay. Be careful.

**Theresa** (*indignant*) I know how to push swings. (*She takes over from* **Dominic**.) You got a girlfriend?

**Dominic** No. You got a boyfriend?

**Theresa** No. (*Of* **Jack**.) He's wet through, in't he?

**Dominic** Where? (*Lifts* **Jack** *out of the swing and inspects him anxiously. He's very wet.*) Oh.

**Theresa** Better get him changed.

**Darren**, *attempting ambitious gymnastics, falls off the swing. No tears.* **Theresa** *goes to him.*

You stupid moron! Come on. Let's have a look at you. (*To* **Dominic**.) I'll have to get him home and all. If he bleeds, it takes ages for it to stop. Somethin' wrong with him. See you. Bye Jack.

**Dominic** (*to* **Jack**) Say 'Bye-bye'.

**Theresa** *and* **Darren** *leave, the boy limping.*

**Dominic** Oh Jack, I'm sorry. Come on, let's get you sorted out. Come on.

*He puts* **Jack** *into his buggy, and hurries with him across the park to the car.*

*Back of* **Philip**'*s shop. The same day. Dusk.*

**Philip**'*s hanging out the washing on the roof. On the street below,* **Dominic**'*s Beetle drives up.* **Dominic** *gets out.* **Philip** *calls from the roof.*

**Philip** Dominic, Marilyn's not back yet.

**Dominic** That's okay.

**Philip** Why don't you come up for a drink?

**Dominic** Jack's asleep. (**Jack** *is in his child's seat in the car.*)

**Philip** That's okay. Leave him in the car. We can watch him from up here.

**Dominic** *goes up the iron steps* (*it's a fire escape.*) *to the rooftop.*

**Dominic** Listen, I'm sorry about this morning.

**Philip** (*still hanging the washing*) Yeah, I'm sorry too.

**Dominic** After all that he got soaked and I had to buy him an entire wardrobe.

**Philip** You should have brought him back.

**Dominic** Well.

**Philip** Apart from that, was it a good day?

**Dominic** Yes, it was fine.

**Philip** Listen, I've still got some more washing to do. (*He indicates the basket.*) So if you've got any of Jack's things, I'll bung them in.

**Dominic** Uh. No, I've left them back at the house. (*Checking himself.*) The room.

**Philip** That's okay.

**Dominic** I mean I've washed them. Well, I put them in to soak. I'm not very good at washing. I'm more of an ironing man, myself.

**Philip** With me it's the opposite. I love hanging out the clothes.

**Dominic** (*mock horror*) Terrible! (*Pause.*) No, listen, what I said earlier was uncalled for. (*Genuine apology.*)

**Philip** Forget it. (*Genuine acceptance.*)

**Dominic**  I've been thinking how much more beautiful Marilyn looks since she's been living here.

**Philip**  (*thinking*)  She always was, I think. (*He is struggling with a large sheet.*)

**Dominic**  Can I give you a hand?

**Philip**  No, it's okay. Why don't you go and check on Jack?

**Dominic**  Right.

*He smiles at* **Philip** *and goes back down the steps.*

*Outside* **Angie/Stephanie** *'s house. A little later.*

**Dominic** *drives up to see* **Chris** *outside the house.* **Chris** *was not expected.*

**Chris**  Hi. Where is everybody?

**Dominic**  What are you doing here?

**Chris**  I'm doing a chopsticks course. Where's the family?

**Dominic**  Jack's gone home. The girls are at a conference. So's Marilyn, as it happens. It's a women's conference.

**Chris**  I see. So. They can compare notes.

**Dominic**  Yeah. That's what I thought. (*A shade impatient.*) What are you doing here?

**Chris**  Stephanie and I are going Chinesing. I thought you and Angie were coming too.

**Dominic**  Chris – Celia's staying with me tonight. I mean, that's the . . . she's coming over, so . . .

**Chris**  Oh.

**Dominic**  Yeah. Oh.

**Chris**  Well, it doesn't matter if we eat, does it?

**Dominic**  Christ. What am I playing at? What am I doing?

**Chris**  (*cheerful*)  I don't know. That's what Stephanie asked me. That's what Siobhan asked me. I expect Angie will ask me later on. Marilyn hasn't got my new phone number, has she? Oh, and I don't know Celia yet.

**Dominic**  Shut up. When did Siobhan ask you? (*Sighs. Notices* **Angie** *and* **Stephanie** *approaching.*) Christ, here they come.

**Stephanie**  Thanks for giving us a lift.

**Dominic**  What?

**Stephanie**  You passed us.

**Dominic**  I'm sorry. I must have been miles away.

**Angie**  Hello Chris. (*She doesn't say hello to* **Dominic**.)

**Chris**  Hi. Hi. Steph. How was your thing?

**Stephanie**  (*brightly*)  Terrific. In fact we decided on the way home we're giving up men.

**Angie** *catches* **Dominic**'*s eye and looks down.*

**Chris**  (*unperturbed*)  When? 'Cause I bought you both a present.

**Stephanie**  Soon. Probably.

**Chris**  Oh, 'soon probably'. That's all right then. These are for you. (*He presents, with a flourish, ornamental black chopsticks. Four pairs.*) Dominic's taking his back.

**Angie**  Oh?

**Dominic**  Yeah, I've got people staying tonight.

**Angie**  Oh.

**Dominic**  I can't really duck out. (*He twiddles his chopsticks.*) I promise I'll practise at home.

*Nobody speaks for a moment. It is tense.*

**Stephanie**  I'm going in. Is anybody else?

**Dominic**  Perhaps I'd better just go straight off.

**Stephanie**  Okay. Chris?

**Chris**  I'd like to. Can I?

**Stephanie**  Possibly.

**Chris**  See you, Dom.

**Stephanie** *and* **Chris** *go in.*

**Angie**  Steph and me are going to the Isle of Wight next weekend.

*A beat.*

**Dominic** Great. Well, should I ring during the week and possibly discuss the following Saturday?

*A beat.*

**Angie** (*quietly; a trace of bitterness, a trace of regret*) It's up to you. (*She turns to go in.*)

**Dominic** (*very gently*) I hope the Isle of Wight's nice. (*Pause.*) See you, then.

**Angie** Bye.

**Dominic** *stands by the gate, watching her go in.*

**Dominic**'s *house. That night.*

**Dominic** *enters, concerned because there is a hall light on. The place is immaculate, polished. He walks cautiously, not sure what's happened. As he passes the door of the sitting room,* **Siobhan** *speaks. She's been sitting on the sofa with some books for her research, waiting for him to return.*

**Siobhan** Dom?

**Dominic** Siobhan? What's going on?

**Siobhan** (*smiling*) I thought I'd spring-clean. Hi. You're back.

**Dominic** Why?

**Siobhan** Why spring-clean? Because there were things growing in your cupboard. Because, with no furniture to settle into, the dust was getting aggressive.

**Dominic** No look, I thought we'd arranged that if I came home I'd come to you?

**Siobhan** Well, now there's no need. 'Thank you Siobhan for spending all day cleaning.' 'It's a pleasure.' (*She curtseys.*)

**Dominic** (*aggressive*) I don't need a domestic. I tried that. I wasn't good at it.

**Siobhan** (*stung*) Right.

**Dominic** (*calming, but still irritated*) No, of course, thank you. Thank you. I just feel embarrassed.

**Siobhan** Well don't. Feel affectionate. Feel sexy, if you like. (*She cuddles him.*) Shall I run a bath? You look worn out.

**Dominic** (*frozen in her arms*)  Actually, the reason I came back was because I had this sudden flash I'd said I'd put some people up for the weekend.

**Siobhan**  Okay. Are you worried about feeding them?

**Dominic**  Feeding her.

**Siobhan**  Are you worried about feeding her?

*A beat.*

**Dominic**  No.

**Siobhan** *unravels herself from the embrace.*

**Siobhan**  Well you can't say fairer than that.

*She picks up her books and leaves. The sound of the front door closing.*

**Dominic**'s *house. Later the same night.*

**Dominic** – *bathed and changed – is preparing the table for a meal. It is carefully laid. He puts a bowl of spinach, avocado and egg salad in the middle. In the bowl are his chopsticks: impromptu salad servers. He uncorks a bottle of wine. He surveys the table. It looks good.*

*The telephone rings. He goes into the hall to answer.*

*The telephone is on the table in the hall where* **Dominic** *and* **Marilyn** *used to keep their joint diary. Above the table is a notice-board. A clutter of reminders, drawings and cards. Photographs of* **Jack** *including one of him wearing the fisherman's smock and* **Angie**'s *hands in evidence. One of* **Dominic** *taken by* **Celia**: *odd, quirky, stylish. Another one, cut from a magazine, of* **Celia**. *It is deliberately concealed by a large notice. As* **Dominic** *talks on the phone, he takes out the drawing pins, revealing* **Celia**'s *photograph.*

**Dominic**  Hello. Yes. Speaking. (*Excited when he realizes who it is.*) Hi, hi Celia! What's the matter – you got lost. (*Pause.*) What? (*Pause. Less excited.*) Oh. (*Pause.*) No, nothing, don't worry about it. (*Pause.*) No, no, no. (*Pause.*) No, I had a salad. No. (*Pause.*) Don't worry. I'll feed it to the cat. (*Pause.*) So. How about next weekend? (*Pause.*) Okay. (*Pause.*) I did. I have an intimate relationship with your answerphone. Did you get my letter? Well, you should be very flattered. I'm normally a 'two lines, love Dominic' man. Yes. (**Celia** *is called away.*) Oh, right. Well, shall I ring you back? (*Pause.*) Oh. (*Pause.*) Okay. Yeah, you too. Bye-bye.

*He replaces the receiver. Realising that she hasn't registered his interest in the slightest, he sits gloomily on the stairs.*

**Marilyn/Philip** *'s bedroom. The same night.*

**Marilyn** *enters from the bathroom. She's surprised to see* **Philip** *in bed: it means* **Jack** *has gone to sleep.*

**Philip** He's asleep.

**Marilyn** I don't believe it. What did you do? Hit him over the head?

**Philip** Only a couple of times.

**Marilyn** Well, I don't know how you do it.

**Philip** (*explains*) I've got no breasts and I sing badly: he gets bored. (*They both smile.*) Tell me about the conference.

**Marilyn** It was great. Tell me about Dominic.

**Philip** No, I want a blow by blow account. Great's not good enough. Dominic was fine.

**Marilyn** *sits on the bed. Then cuddles him, her head on his chest. They're close. In love.*

**Marilyn** Oh, by the way. I'm not pregnant.

**Philip** Oh.

**Marilyn** *looks up just too late to see the disappointment on his face. She gives him a kiss.*

**Siobhan** *'s house. The next day (Sunday). Early evening.*

**Siobhan** *opens the door on a penitent* **Dominic**. *She is appropriately unwelcoming. They stand on the doorstep.*

**Dominic** I got stood up. (*No response.*) Do you want to share a salad? (*He holds up a shopping bag.*)

**Siobhan** No, thanks. (*Pause.*) Do I want to share you? No, thanks.

**Dominic** (*honest*) That figures. Listen Siobhan, I wanted to say a few things . . . (*He can't think how to say them.*) I mean, well I've been seeing someone in Bristol . . . uh . . .

**Siobhan** I know.

**Dominic** Do you?

**Siobhan** Chris told me. He didn't tell me, but he couldn't say no when I asked.

**Dominic** Right. I'm not going to be able to say anything, am I?

**Siobhan** Not today, Dom. No.

**Dominic** Tomorrow?

**Siobhan** I doubt it, Dom.

**Dominic** Tuesday? Wednesday? Stop me, you know, if I'm getting warm. (*Nothing.*) Next weekend? (*Nothing.*) Right. (*He retreats to the gate.*)

**Siobhan** (*meaning it*) Take care.

**Dominic** (*meaning it*) Yeah. And you.

*He watches as she shuts the front door.*


**Dominic**'s *house. A Wednesday some weeks later.*

*If anything the house is even more stark.* **Dominic** *has jettisoned virtually all of the furniture.* **Jack** *is asleep in his buggy in the hall.* **Marilyn** *sits at the table in the kitchen/dining room.* **Dominic** *enters with a box.*

**Dominic** I keep forgetting to bring these back.

**Marilyn** (*examining the contents*) What is it?

**Dominic** Well, various bits of junk, really. It's yours, not mine, though. I'll shove it in the car for you.

**Marilyn** Okay. Though I don't know where it's all going to go.

**Dominic** Well.

**Marilyn** Seems a bit ridiculous.

**Dominic** What?

**Marilyn** The house. It's so empty. And the place in Bristol's not really big enough. What have you done with the sofa?

**Dominic** (*smiles*) Oxfam.

**Marilyn** (*smiles*) That's where it came from.

**Dominic** That's where it's gone back to.

**Marilyn** *gets up and walks through to the sitting room.* **Dominic** *follows.*

**Dominic** Don't let me forget to give you the documents for the car.

**Marilyn** Right. Thanks.

**Dominic** I think you'll have to get someone to look at the exhaust.

**Marilyn** Right. (*She moves to the window. Looks at the house opposite.*) Do you see much of Frank and Annabel?

**Dominic** Oh no. Nothing. Well, no: at first they came over. They asked for your address. Did they write?

**Marilyn** Yes. A card. It was kind.

**Dominic** Yeah. I sometimes see Frank. You know, he has this habit of materialising every time a woman comes within twenty feet of the house. (*Laughs. A pause.*) Oh yeah, and I had some of their home-made wine, which I gave to my father. I think he gives it to someone else.

**Marilyn** Oxfam.

**Dominic** (*smiles*) Probably. (*Pause.*) Well. This is terribly normal. (*He means the conversation.*)

**Marilyn** Is that a regular event?

**Dominic** What's that?

**Marilyn** Women coming within twenty feet of the house.

**Dominic** Um . . . it happens.

**Marilyn** The girl from the restaurant?

**Dominic** No. (*Pause.*) No. (*Pause.*) You're right – this house is ridiculous. I wanted to empty it and I've forgotten why. Anyway, I'm going to sell it. I'm going to move. (*Pause.*) Because there's no chance of you coming back.

**Marilyn** No. I don't think there is.

**Dominic** You know, what's funny is that you and Philip seem the couple now. I tried to imagine you naked the other day. I couldn't. (*Pause.*) Or touching you. (**Jack** *cries.*) We have a waking baby, I think.

**Marilyn**  I'll go. (*As she goes out to the hall.*) I thought I was pregnant again.

**Dominic**  Oh. Are you?

**Marilyn**  (*coming back with* **Jack** *in her arms*)  No.

**Dominic**  (*cooing*)  Here he is!

**Marilyn**  Say, 'Hello, Dad.'

**Dominic**  (*after a beat*)  D'you fancy a walk, Marilyn?

**Marilyn**  Uh. Where?

**Dominic**  I don't know. The park.

**Marilyn**  Okay.


*The park. A little later.*

**Dominic** *and* **Marilyn** *push* **Jack** *into the park. It is busy. Mostly just mums and kids.*

*If you were watching from a distance, you'd see a happy couple with their child. Laughing about something. The father pulling the baby out of the pushchair, sitting him on one end of the see-saw, and holding him while mother and child gently bump and rise alternately. You'd see the mother getting on the roundabout with the baby. The father pushing them round. Then jumping on himself. Then showing off, holding on with only one hand and leaning out as the roundabout turns.*

*And round and round they spin.*